DISCONTINUITY
IN GREEK CIVILIZATION

THE J. H. GRAY LECTURES FOR 1965

DISCONTINUITY
IN GREEK CIVILIZATION

BY

RHYS CARPENTER

*Professor Emeritus of Classical Archaeology in
Bryn Mawr College, Pennsylvania*

CAMBRIDGE
AT THE UNIVERSITY PRESS
1966

Published by The Syndics of the Cambridge University Press
Bentley House, 200 Euston Road, London N.W. 1
American Branch: 32 East 57th Street, New York, N.Y. 10022
West African Office: P.M.B. 5181, Ibadan, Nigeria

Library of Congress Catalogue Card Number: 66–23109

Printed in Great Britain
at the University Printing House, Cambridge
(Brooke Crutchley, University Printer)

CONTENTS

v

FOREWORD

From Plato's Timaeus[1]

Now listen, Sokrates, to a story which, though passing strange, is nevertheless entirely true, even as Solon, wisest of the Seven Sages, once asserted. Know that Solon was a relative and intimate friend of my great-grandfather Dropides, as he himself says many times in his poems. Now Solon told my grandfather Kritias (as the old man used to recall to us) that our city had performed marvellous deeds in ancient times, but these had been lost to mind through lapse of time and extinction of life.

This, then, is the olden story as I heard it from a very old man; for my grandfather (as he said) was already then close to his ninetieth year, while I myself was somewhere about ten years old ...

In Egypt in the Delta, at whose apex the stream of the Nile divides, there is a province called the Saitic Nome, and the largest city of this province is Sais—from which also came King Amasis ... The inhabitants are extremely well disposed toward us of Athens ... and Solon when he visited them was held in high honour. Now, specifically, when he made inquiry about the past from the priests most versed in such matters, he found that neither he nor any other Greek really knew anything at all about it. And when he tried to tell them of our own remotest antiquity, one of the priests, an extremely aged man, said, 'Solon, Solon, you Greeks are eternal children! There is not a single grown-up among you.'

[1] The speaker is Plato's maternal uncle, Kritias the Younger.

On hearing this, Solon asked, 'What do you mean by that?'! Whereat the priest replied, 'You are all of you young of mind because you possess no ancient lore, no knowledge hoar with time. And the cause thereof is this:

'There have been many occasions of human destruction, and there will be many more. The chiefest source of these is fire and water;[1] but countless lesser ones have been due to other causes. The legend that is told among you also, how Phaethon, child of the Sun, once yoked his father's car but, being unable to guide it on its wonted course, burnt up the earth beneath him and was himself destroyed by lightning—all this, though told in mythic guise, is true, inasmuch as a deviation of the celestial bodies moving past the earth does, at long intervals, cause destruction of earthly things through burning heat . . .

'So this is the reason why among us here oldest traditions still prevail and whenever anything great or glorious or otherwise noteworthy occurs, it is written down and preserved in our temples; whereas among you and other nations that chance to be but recently endowed with the art of writing and civilized needs, at stated turn of years there has recurred like a plague brought down upon you a celestial current, leaving only an unlettered and uncivilized remnant; wherefore you have to begin all over again like children, without knowledge of what has taken place in older times either in our land or in yours . . . Consequently you are unaware that the finest and bravest of mortal races once inhabited your land, from whom you and your fellow citizens are descended through the

1 *Sc.* drought and flood.

meagre human seed that survived. Nothing do you know thereof, because of the many intervening generations silent for lack of written speech.'

There follows an account of how this 'finest and bravest of mortal races' defeated in battle the waxing power of the kingdom of Atlantis, a huge continental island in the ocean beyond the Gibraltar Strait; and how, after its armies had been defeated by the Athenians, it came to an unexpected and terrible end, about which Kritias had heard only that:

Some time thereafter there came tremendous earthquakes and overwhelming floods. And in a single terrible day and night all your armies were engulfed and the island of Atlantis likewise sank and disappeared beneath the sea.

1

A CLIMATIC BACKGROUND
TO HISTORY

No one doubts that the earth's climate has undergone important changes in the past. The series of ice ages that have come and gone is sufficient proof of this. But such long-term fluctuations were ascribed to remote geologic rather than to human time, until recent investigation brought a different perspective and it became certain that the last ice age had ended only a few thousand years ago—twelve thousand, to be specific. By 7000 B.C. Europe and North America had become as ice-free as they are today. But it is not correct to assume that, once the great ice sheets over the continents melted away, the whole earth's climate grew steadily warmer, as though a huge planetary refrigerator were being defrosted. On the contrary, pollen analysis of the peatbogs of northern Europe revealed that some seven thousand years ago that region must have enjoyed a climate considerably warmer than that of more recent time; and during the subsequent millennia there have been several recurrences of decidedly colder conditions. In short, as a leading climatological authority once expressed it, 'the unvarying climate of history is evidently a myth'. Marked alterations in climatic states thus belong not merely to geologic aeons but to actual human experience in the past; and we know of at least two regressions in human civilization that may be directly ascribed to climatic change.

While the ice sheet was still spread over northern Europe, extending south almost as far as London and Paris, the glaciers and snowfields of Switzerland still farther south, being larger than at present, threw a formidable barrier across the southern part of the continent. Between these two impassable fronts—the solid ice to the north and the snowblocked mountains to the south—a corridor of open country led west from inner Asia to the Atlantic coast. At the end of this corridor, in what today is France, where the winds brought moisture from the unfrozen Atlantic and somewhat tempered the rigours of the atmosphere, there lived a race of hunters amid the herds of wild animals—reindeer and bison and mammoth—on which they fed. All that we know about this rude and hardy folk has been learned by exploring the caves in which they took shelter and in which they have left us the bones of the animals which they ate, some of the tools which they made from such bone and, remarkable beyond all, the superb coloured drawings of the animals that they hunted. These cave paintings have been copied, photographed, reproduced in black-and-white and in colour so frequently that they are by now familiar to a wide public; but it is probably only the professional student of prehistory who knows what happened to these ancient hunters of twelve and more thousand years ago and what sort of human society took their place. For nothing endures forever, and the cavemen's happy hunting ground faded away with the melting of the ice.

One might suppose that, as the summers gradually grew warmer and the ice cap receded, human existence would have become easier. But the new warmth and the increased moisture altered the steppe-like grazing grounds of the animals on which the hunters depended for food and raiment. Scrub growth gave way to forest; swamps and marshland replaced the open pastures. In search of the old way of life to which they were accustomed, the animals (and after them the hunters) seem to have wandered away under the climatic shelter of the retreating ice cap through the great European corridor across Russia into Siberia, where we lose sight of them. Those of the hunters who stayed behind had to adapt themselves to new and less bountiful conditions, snaring and trapping and fishing. Compared with the abundant life of the great-game hunting days, this was an impoverished sort of existence, since the secrets of ploughing and sowing and of animal breeding were as yet unknown. Artistic skill disappeared; craftsmanship diminished; all life had to be lived on a meaner level of subsistence. This was the first great cultural recession of which we have certain evidence and of which we can confidently say that it was caused primarily by a climatic change.

The next occurrence was surprisingly different and to those who have never examined the evidence, hardly credible. It centres on the formation of the great North African desert known to us as the Sahara and as large as the whole of continental Europe. Improbable as it may seem, the melting of the ice cap over northern Europe at the close of the last ice age occasioned the transformation of vast stretches of flourishing pasture land in North Africa, far away from the ice, into a waterless and barely habitable waste. As the ice retreated in northern Europe, the desert expanded in Africa.

1-2

How was this possible?

The prime cause of this astonishing transformation was the ever-blowing trade wind; for it is the trade wind that creates and maintains the desert zones in the northern and southern tropics that girdle our planet's continental regions. Where this persistent rush of air crosses the oceans it leaves no recognizable mark of its passing; but where it streams overland it leaves aridity in its wake through a zone as much as a thousand miles wide. At the two confines of the wasteland that it creates, the trade wind begins and again ceases abruptly, as though coming from nowhere and journeying nowhither. But there is here no mystery; for it begins its course by descending from far aloft and ends it by rising skyward again, leaving beneath it the equatorial calm of the doldrums. The mechanism of this seemingly unmotivated behaviour is well understood. The heating power of the overhead equatorial sun creates as it were a vast chimney of upward climbing warm wet air. On reaching the colder upper atmosphere this sheds most of its moisture through condensation, to produce the rainfall of the equatorial regions. But the air itself, drained of most of its water, cannot descend against the unceasing upward draught up the 'chimney' and so is forced to drift away over the roof of the world, northward and southward toward the poles. However, it cannot complete its poleward journey because it encounters the so-called 'polar front' in the temperate latitudes, which blocks its progress and forces it to descend. As it does so, it becomes steadily warmer (and therewith drier) under the increasing pressure of the atmosphere until, on nearing the earth's surface, it divides into a pole current that starts the cyclonic rain-storms of the temperate zones spinning, while most of the great draught of air returns equatorward. It is this unceasing return draught which constitutes the trade wind. Growing steadily warmer as it moves through lower latitudes, it will pick up moisture but cannot condense it to drop rain on the lands over which it blows. As a result the trade wind will desiccate entire regions, into which rain-laden storms from other quarters can so seldom penetrate that all but the hardiest vegetation must wither. Since the belt of the trade wind is roughly a thousand miles wide, we should not be surprised that this is the average extent of the Sahara desert from north to south.

It should be carefully observed that this great circulatory atmospheric system is not tied to the geographic equatorial line but to the position of the sun relative to the earth; so that, as the sun moves north and south in the sky during the year, the trade-wind belt in either hemisphere will move responsively, although with much lesser range. In the northern hemisphere, and specifically in the eastern Mediterranean, during late July and August the belt of the trade winds shifts north with the summer sun until its régime of rainless weather covers the Aegean. Accordingly it would be entirely accurate to say that during the summer of every year the climate of the Sahara prevails over most of Hellas.

During the ice age climatic conditions in the Mediterranean basin must have been very markedly different from those of later time. V. Gordon Childe stated the situation briefly and vividly, as I here transcribe the pertinent passage from his *The Most Ancient East*:

Discontinuity in Greek Civilization

While Northern Europe was covered in ice as far as the Harz, and the Alps and the Pyrenees were capped with glaciers, the Arctic high pressure deflected southwards the Atlantic rainstorms. The cyclones that today traverse Central Europe then passed over the Mediterranean Basin and the Northern Sahara and continued, undrained by Lebanon, across Mesopotamia and Arabia to Persia and India. The parched Sahara enjoyed a regular rainfall, and farther east the showers were not only more bountiful than today but were distributed over the whole year, instead of being restricted to winter ... We should expect in North Africa, Arabia, Persia and the Indus Valley parklands and savannahs, such as flourish today north of the Mediterranean.

In brief, during an ice age there should not have been any desert where the Sahara is today. Geologists, zoologists, and ethnologists all agree that this was indeed the case.

The geologists say that rivers were running fullstream, carving out the gorges and stream-beds whose dry courses may be seen today. The zoologists say that tropical varieties of fish and aquatic animals such as crocodiles and hippopotami made their way up these now dried-up rivers, to live and reproduce themselves in what is now the very heart of the desert. The ethnologists report that on the rocks which once were the walls of water-filled gorges there are engraved drawings of giraffes and elephants, crocodiles and leopards, and other animals such as do not exist, and could not survive, in the present environment

But when the great ice sheet retreated over northern Europe, there in well-watered North Africa some 1,500 miles from the nearest edge of the ice cap, where there

6

had never been glaciers of any size, there was an astonishing climatic repercussion for which the only possible explanation is that, as the European ice melted back toward the arctic, the polar front moved back with it and the zone of the trade wind expanded, thereby creating the desert that exists today.

The peculiar thing about the formation of deserts is that the process seems to start a sort of chain reaction, easier to set in motion than to stop or throw in reverse. This makes it very difficult to determine at just what period in the twelve thousand years since the last ice age dissipated, the Saharan region—which is nowadays so nearly uninhabitable that it ranks as the most sparsely settled region of the earth next to the Antarctic—became desiccated to such a degree that men and most of the larger animals were forced to move out. By 7000 B.C. Europe was practically ice-free except for those glaciers which, then as now, clung to the higher or more northerly mountain ranges. By that date, therefore, it seems reasonable to suppose that the zone of the rainless trade wind had assumed pretty much its present location and extent, so that rainfall in North Africa would have been reduced approximately to the present-day minimum. Thus, while in Europe the steppeland and the snowfields were giving place to forest and swampland, the trend in North Africa was exactly the opposite, from open grass-covered uplands and mountains full of lakes and rivers to arid stretches of rock and gravel, dry river-beds and sandy flats. The great shifting dunes of windblown sand, of which we are apt to think when we picture the Sahara in our minds, must have come later, since they would take many centuries to form and even today occupy less than a sixth of the whole Sahara zone. But whether sand or merely dry riverbed and parched pastureland, the result was calamitous for living things. Little by little, as the Sahara gained in grimness, men and animals were forced out.

Meanwhile to the east beyond the Red Sea a similar event was taking place in Arabia where, along the same latitude and from the same natural cause, a second and smaller area (though, even so, considerably larger than Europe west of the Iron Curtain) was likewise turning to desert and forcing its inhabitants to migrate. Here then were two great reservoirs of well-established humanity that could no longer offer food and water for more than a small fraction of their erstwhile population. From the desert of Arabia came forth the Semites; from the desert of North Africa were dispersed the Hamites, moving in all available directions to occupy new lands. This great exodus from the Sahara and Central Arabia is the second discoverable instance of a momentous impact of climatic change.

Herewith (it is generally assumed) the epochal examples of man's response to climatic upheaval came to an end, since nothing comparable in magnitude to the passing of an ice age has happened since. Man, along with nature, is supposed to have settled down to an orderly climatic régime, disturbed by nothing more drastic than the annual change of the seasons and the daily uncertainty of the weather. Such a view is entirely wrong. To quote a leading historian of climate, 'The present day does not differ from the past; variations of climate are still in progress, similar in kind, though not in extent, to the climatic vicissitudes of the ice-age.'

This being so, we are entitled to shift attention from geologic to historic time, to inquire whether there are adequate grounds for postulating that the trade wind which today brings drought to Saharan North Africa has at any times during the comparatively recent past extended its parching effect farther north, to assail Greece with aridity.

The primary proposition is extremely simple: if in the past the size of the North European ice cap has directly influenced the size of the North African desert (in the sense that this desert zone has widened as the ice retreated northward), this process should continue on a small scale as well as on a large one, and hence should still be operative whenever the glaciated portions of our planet expand or decrease. During the past ten thousand years, after the bulk of ice age glaciation had melted in Europe, there have been demonstrably periods of considerably greater warmth than at present, alternating at other times with periods of returning cold. The crucial question is whether this has been happening on a large enough scale to produce any climatic alteration capable of affecting human history. One may be inclined to object that, since these fluctuations probably did not involve an increase or decrease of more than 2 or 3 or possibly 4° Fahrenheit in the overall daily average temperature of our planet, they might have discommoded or gratified our remote ancestors, but hardly forced them to change their habits or their habitations. But to raise this objection is to misunderstand the possible effect of even small increases in planetary temperature on the specific area in which we are here interested. For the primary issue is not the state of mean annual temperature in the Aegean or elsewhere, but the behaviour of the trade wind and the course of the temperate storm tracks during periods of diminished planetary glaciation. To determine this—be it frankly admitted—is by no means an easy or simple problem.

If at first hearing one is inclined to be sceptical about the effects of a northward shift of the Saharan drought zone into southern Europe, he should consider that the question at issue is the potential northward reach of this expansion, and not its actual existence as a disturbing climatic factor. For—as previously explained—each summer as the sun travels north in the sky, what we might term the earth's heat equator is displaced northward, so that the operation of the trade wind shifts—although by no means to an equal extent. Whereas the sun moves through some $23\frac{1}{2}°$ of latitude, the trade wind following the summer sun shifts through approximately no more than $10°$; but this is equivalent to a northward displacement of nearly 700 miles. Accordingly the rainless régime of the Sahara moves north beyond Africa during every July and August to cover the islands of Cyprus and Crete and the southern Aegean. In Attica and on the Cyclades there are so few showers between late May and September that the year's vegetation withers and dies and the skies grow hazy and dull. By adapting themselves to these conditions nature and man survive successfully; but were the rainless zone to spread farther and endure longer each year, the resulting effect on human and animal ecology might assume extremely serious proportions.

Specifically, if the trade-wind zone were to move farther north, following the retreating polar front incident to a general rise in planetary temperature, the storm tracks along which rain is presently conveyed eastward across the European continent should suffer displacement toward the north, thereby leaving the Mediterranean subject to the prevailing westerly winds, whose orographic condensation of moisture evaporated from the sea would accrue only to the western-exposed slopes of the mountainous lands in their path, leaving the interior tracts of land consistently dry during most months of the year.

I intend to pursue this argument more explicitly in my final lecture. Meanwhile it is more pertinent to inquire whether professional investigators of climatic change postulate the occurrence of warm phases during historic time sufficiently pronounced to induce the phenomenon just described, and, if so, whether the approximate dates which they assign to these phases synchronize with any retrogression in human civilization that written history or material archaeology establish for the Mediterranean world.

To deal with this latter evidence first, leaving the meteorological evidence for later examination, it may be asserted with entire confidence that in the course of the past three millennia there are discoverable at least two instances of catastrophic decline in human well-being and cultural attainment centred on the eastern Mediterranean. These took place at an interval of about 1,800 years. Whether they were preceded by other similar crises at approximately the same interval of time cannot, on the strength of presently available evidence, be determined with any degree of certainty.

Since it lies beyond the immediate scope of these lectures, I can touch only very briefly on the latest in this presumptive series of cultural retrogressions in the Mediterranean, even though it deserves much more extensive treatment in view of the extent to which it is ignored by handbooks dealing with the period. If it is discussed at all, its terrible toll of human misfortune is generally ascribed to disastrous contemporary events of a political or politico-economic kind. But in most histories of the Mediterranean the seventh century after Christ is largely a blank; and of this blank in cultural history I have myself had some experience while digging on the site of ancient Corinth. There the American excavators have more than once dug down through the unimportant Turkish level beneath the present surface and encountered a flourishing layer of Byzantine occupation attributable to the eleventh and twelfth centuries after Christ. Below this, if a second and older Byzantine level is met before the period of late Roman imperial rule is reached, that level will invariably belong to the fifth and sixth centuries. Except for an occasional stray coin, the seventh and eighth centuries are missing. What went wrong in the seventh century that it should have left no trace? Some historians would say that the gap is due to the invasion of Greece by half-civilized Slavic hordes. But these do not seem ever to have reached Corinth; and on closer examination the Slavic conquest turns out to have been chiefly a sporadic unwarlike penetration by nomad shepherd bands moving in with their families, animals, and household goods, not so much conquering as refilling an empty land. A Byzantine chronicler confirms this by remarking that 'Greece was slavicized after the plague had depopulated the world'. Plague there was, certainly, and starvation; but these are calamities that may have a climatic cause. Other historians maintain that it was the Arab pirates who pillaged and thus depopulated seventh-century Greece. But the country can be proved to have been just as empty in regions where the Saracens never set foot.

Elsewhere in the eastern Mediterranean there are signs of similar catastrophe. In the heart of Turkey there is a region called today 'the 1001 churches' with the same exaggeration that has bestowed on the famous collection of Arab stories the inaccurate title of 'The 1001 Nights'. But while there never were a thousand churches there, the number of them built during the fifth and sixth centuries of our era testifies to a very sizeable population. But during and after the seventh century no more churches were built and those already built were allowed to go to ruin. Today they stand empty and desolate. Who killed off their congregations? The Arabs and after them the Seljuk Turks, say the historians; but the chances are better than even that here again the historians are wrong. The real enemy seems to have been the failure of the local water supply, due to a lack of adequate rainfall over a long period.

Farther to the east in Syria there is an even more spectacular assembly of early Christian stone churches, testifying to an extensive population during the fourth

and fifth centuries, but likewise implying abandonment
and collapse during and after the seventh century. What
caused the catastrophe? The Moslems of the Arab conquest, say the political historians. Yet the Arab subjection
does not seem to have been so bloodthirsty. 'Not a single
Syrian town was captured by force of arms', says a recent
student of the period; 'all accepted the easy and generous
terms of the Arab chieftains: Jew, Samaritan, and Christian
alike welcomed the Arabs as their deliverers from Greek
oppression.' What then caused desolation amid the stone
churches? It was the drying up of the springs through
failure in the annual rain supply, without which neither
man nor beast nor growing vegetation can survive.

Before I turn back to the earlier and even more disastrous cultural depression in Mediterranean civilization,
I shall make an apparent digression which in reality is no
digression but is wholly relevant. Even while the Mediterranean was suffering the setback which I have illus-
trated for Greece and Turkey and Syria, northern Europe
was prospering. Although we refer to the period from the
seventh to the eleventh century as the Dark Ages,
civilization was on the upgrade in France and Germany
and Britain. The English climate seems to have been
exceptionally mild, if we may so conclude from the report
that grapes could be ripened and wine made—a feat im-
possible in Roman times. In Ireland the monasteries
reached a height of prosperity and learning unequalled
until then. In Scandinavia the population had increased
to the overflow colonization level by the ninth century.
During the following decades there began the great
stream of Norse emigration to Iceland and to Greenland

beyond. This latter name is apt to strike us as a rather grim joke; but at the time of settlement the coast was green enough with vegetation to merit such a name. Not until the late thirteenth century did polar ice close in on the lower Greenland coast, as the climate worsened. By the end of the fourteenth century conditions had become so unfavourable that the white men had to retire from the land, to be replaced by Eskimos from the Arctic. But now in our own time the northern ice cover has been melting back, in a spectacular (though perhaps only temporary) retreat, revealing the cemeteries of the old Norse colonists.

What has this to do with the previous discussion? At first glance very little; but if we consider the timetable of events, we find that the bad centuries in the Mediterranean have been good centuries farther north, while the inclement centuries in the north had been favourable to man in the south; for it was just when the northern seas began to freeze shut again after A.D. 1000 and during the stormy phase from the twelfth to the fourteenth centuries that civilization in and about the Mediterranean resumed the great upswing that carried it through the Renaissance into modern times.

This, then, may be the great climatic cycle by which the career of European civilization has been controlled.

I am turning back to much earlier times to the central foci of civilization before the emergence of classical Greece. The calendar time is 1200 B.C., and Mediterranean man has begun to suffer the most severe cultural recession which history records or archaeology can determine. Great kingdoms have collapsed without apparent adequate reason; and the eastern sea shores are overrun by fugitives seeking to force their way into lands less smitten by disaster. In Greece the well-fortified Mycenaean palaces are burned and abandoned; but no one seems to know who burned them. In the heart of the Anatolian plateau the dynasty of Hittite kings, who had treated on equal terms with the pharaohs of Egypt, abruptly comes to an end. Their capital city is abandoned.

What has happened? Nobody offers any valid explanation. The Egyptian records for a few years earlier speak of a severe famine in the Hittite land and of shipments of grain sent in aid by the pharaoh. And some recently published correspondence between Hatti and Syrian Ugarit speaks of a shipment of 2,000 measures of grain to be conveyed in an Ugarit ship as 'a matter of life or death: let the king of Ugarit not linger!'

In Greece the wealth and splendour of the Mycenaean Age vanished utterly, to be succeeded by those miserable centuries of hand-to-mouth existence of which Thucydides seems to have had some hearsay knowledge when he wrote that, long before his day, Greece had been 'without commerce, without communication by land or sea, cultivating no more acreage than the necessities of life demanded, destitute of capital, building no large towns nor attaining any form of greatness'. To which vivid picture we may add that Greece had become illiterate (even as the old Egyptian priest was reported to have told Solon in Plato's *Timaeus*). There is no surer indication of cultural collapse than the failure to transmit the use of letters once this use has been acquired.

What had happened?

Historians have made their usual suggestions—foreign

invaders, barbarian hordes overwhelming the eastern Mediterranean; in Mycenaean Greece the Dorians, driving down from the Albanian highlands; in Asia Minor the Phrygians, crossing from the Balkan highlands. But archaeology does not bear out these explanations. Like the Slavs in the Middle Ages when the climatic cycle had run full circle, the Dorian Greeks seem to have moved into a depopulated land, bringing their wives and children and goods and chattels in a haphazard and unwarlike migration. And in Asia Minor the Hittites seem to have deserted their ancestral sites and moved south-east through the mountains into northern Syria centuries before the Phrygians ferried themselves across the Bosporus and took possession. South of the central plateau 'the coasts were restless', according to a contemporary Egyptian record much quoted in recent years; 'no land withstood them . . . they came with fire before them, onward against Egypt'. They were met and repulsed by the alarmed pharaoh in what he boasted was a tremendous victory. But what set this motley crowd in motion? No one knows—unless it was hunger that drove them; for they came not as lone raiders, but with their wives and children, by ship and by oxcart.

So it was, from one end of the Mediterranean to the other. Even Egypt, which had resisted the attack of the shorelanders, lost its vigour and sank into a helpless apathy that was to last for a full four hundred years before at last she roused herself in new energy and brought back some semblance of the proud great Egypt of old days.

No competent historian today doubts the seriousness of this major recession of civilization, a recession which spread from one end of the Mediterranean to the other at the close of the thirteenth century and lasted, with only occasional and very local remission, until the ninth century B.C. It was a widespread collapse of prosperity and power such as would be difficult to parallel from any other place or period in man's civilized career. Yet no one has offered any adequate explanation for its occurrence.

To my thinking, after puzzling for many years over this, the greatest still unsolved problem in Mediterranean history, there is only one solution that will meet all the varied aspects of the case, and that answer is—*famine*, a dropping of the food supply below the critical level for subsistence. And by famine I do not mean an occasional failure of several consecutive harvests, but such an enduring and disastrous destruction of the annual yield as only a drastic climatic change could have occasioned.

But what proof have we that such a climatic change actually overwhelmed the Mediterranean lands about 1200 B.C. and lasted through several centuries until, around 850 B.C., a climate returned more favourable to human existence? How can we tell what climatic conditions prevailed in a past so far removed and seemingly so inaccessible to examination?

A number of very different avenues of approach yield intriguing glimpses into the earth's climatic history. These give us pictures that are not always in sharp chronological focus and tend to blur their definition; but by and large they agree so well with one another that there is no valid reason for refusing to accept them. Thus, pollen analysis of north and central European peat bogs has been employed for deducing from their stratified traces of arboreal populations the sequence of climatic variation in prevailing temperature and rainfall, with pertinent approximate dates supplied by prehistoric artefacts discovered at the various levels. Again, detailed study of the visible traces of past levels of various central European lakes has suggested a climatic past that involved a 'high-water catastrophe' following a period of drought that prevailed until after the close of the second millennium B.C. and was succeeded by a renewed onset of abundant rainfall. Along similar lines of investigation, the past advances and retreats of the European mountain glaciers and polar ice sheets have been interrogated, albeit with indifferent yield of chronological precision for remoter centuries; while, with more immediate reference to human history, the degree of facility of communication across alpine passes has been cited as evidence for regional climata. In North America scrutiny of the ring growth of unusually longliving trees such as sequioa and Douglas fir has served to establish the local incidence of drought and rainfall since the early centuries of the Christian era.

But none of these various techniques seems to have been intensively applied to the Mediterranean zone, a region for which a hitherto unexploited kind of evidence can be turned to account:

As everyone must be aware, the total quantity of water on our planet remains constant for the simple reason that none of it can escape into outer space. But it is unceasingly being converted from its predominant liquid state, now into mobile atmospheric vapour by evaporation, now into earthbound immobility by freezing into ice and snow. If we leave out of consideration the water suspended in the atmosphere in invisible vapour or visible cloud, as being probably a fairly constant total quantity, and consider the remainder in the oceans, lakes and rivers of the earth and in the icefields of the arctics and the glaciers of the higher mountains, we shall find it in self-adjusting equilibrium. As the ice and snow melt and their water runs to the sea, the ocean level rises all over the world; while with contrary result, as glaciers and polar ice caps increase, the oceans lose just that much water and their world-wide level sinks commensurably. This is not exactly surprising, since it is entirely obvious. What is surprising is the scale on which this interaction occurs. After repeated estimates, checked and rechecked, scientists have reached the conclusion that at the height of the last ice age so much of the planetary water was heaped over the land in frozen state that the general ocean level sank some 300 feet! Looking in the other direction they have been speculating what would happen if all the earth's covering of ice were to melt away. How much would the ocean level be lifted? Until recently their calculations favoured a figure around 90 to 100 feet. But new methods for testing the depth of the ice caps overlying Greenland and the Antarctic by seismic reflection (comparable to deep-sea sounding by radar) have shown that previous estimates were much too low and that the polar ice is so thick that, if it were all melted, enough water would be released to raise the planetary water level rather more than 200 feet higher than the present shore line.

Of course, such conclusions are widely popularized in sensational manner; and since another 200 feet of sea water would leave Venice with only its campanile emerging, would drown all of Metropolitan London's central area, submerge New York to the higher floors of its skyscrapers, and convert the European and American seaside resorts into underwater aquaria, all of this would prove distinctly upsetting if it were liable to happen in our lifetime or were to come on with appreciable suddenness. But of course that is not the kind of phenomenon that is envisaged. As a result of the rapid retreat of most of the glaciers in our northern hemisphere during the past half century, the level of the Atlantic does not seem to have risen more than a few inches; and in any event there is no prospect of the disappearance of the polar ice caps in any foreseeable future period of time. Although personally I am convinced that Venice is surely and irremediably doomed to submergence beneath the sea, I do not expect anyone in the present audience to live long enough to enter St Mark's in a gondola—and this despite the fact that more than once in recent years gondolas have been seen navigating the piazza from the flooded piazzetta. As evidence that the level of the Adriatic has risen since the city was first established in the shallow Adriatic lagoons we should consider that the pavement of the piazzetta had to be raised 2½ feet in the sixteenth century, thereby hiding from view the bases of the colonnade of the Doge's Palace (which explains the otherwise inexplicable stumpiness of its columns).

However Venice may have fared and may yet fare, the rise and fall of the world's ocean levels as the earth's accumulation of ice thaws or freezes is real enough; and in consequence the level of planetary water is an index of the general climatic conditions prevailing at the time—even though the calibration of planetary temperature to planetary ocean level may be a technical task of considerable difficulty.

Now, the geologists and the physicists may run into unsurmountable difficulties in trying to determine the exact planetary water level for any given date in the past; but it is possible that the archaeologist can help them out. For the Mediterranean, which is his hunting ground, is not a land-locked sea but, because it is open to the Atlantic through the wide Gibraltar strait, keeps step with the rise and fall of the outside ocean. By fixing his attention on man's occupation of the Mediterranean shoreland during the last three to four thousand years, the archaeologist may be able to discover where the water level stood and thence infer what the overall climatic conditions were for many of the crucial periods of human history. Some specific examples will illustrate what I have in mind.

In Italy at Pozzuoli near the mouth of the bay of Naples, there are remains of the old Roman harbour works which marked that port as the leading maritime station in the Mediterranean. These remains include brick and concrete buttresses which once supported an arcading for a dock or breakwater. On some of these the metal rings for fastening ships' hawsers are still in place; but they are seven feet below the present water level. Since no one ties ships to underwater rings but to moorings at least three or four feet above the water, it seems that at the time when these rings were put in place (probably close to the year A.D. 140) the level of the Mediterranean was some ten feet lower than it is today. But some of these same piers have been attacked by marine borers, such as are still to be found in the bay of Naples; and the pittings and perforations made by these shellfish, which never emerge from the sea, extend up the piers for almost ten feet into the air. Hence it would seem that, at some period between Roman times and our own, the level of the Mediterranean has been ten feet higher than it is now. There is thus in this one spot a record of fluctuation of twenty feet in the earth's ocean level in the past 1,800 years.

Perhaps you wonder why this has not been noticed before. It has been noticed; but the routine explanation has been advanced that, since the bay of Naples is a volcanic region, it is the land and not the water that has been moving up and down. Considered in isolation for this one spot, such an assumption is entirely plausible, since there is no doubt that in many parts of the earth the land has been slowly rising or sinking. But there is similar archaeological evidence from one end of the Mediterranean to the other; and since it can scarcely be supposed that all the Mediterranean shoreland has been moving up and down simultaneously, the only reasonable explanation must be that the water and not the land has been changing level. Evidence of a rise of the sea since the classical period exists along the Sicilian and the North African shore in the western basin of the Mediterranean; and in the eastern basin it may be detected at Greek mainland sites, some of the Aegean islands, and along the southern coast of Turkey.

The tiny island of Pantaleo in a lagoon off the western tip of Sicily is the site of the erstwhile Carthaginian colony

of Motya. A stone causeway connecting it with the mainland still survives, but now lies under several feet of sea
water—not because its higher courses have been removed,
but because the general water level has risen above it. A
similar phenomenon may be observed in the gulf of
Gabes where, close to the shore of southern Tunisia, the
large and fertile island of Jerba was once connected with
the African mainland by a causeway (presumably con-
structed in Roman times) which today lies submerged
under several feet of water.

In the eastern basin of the Mediterranean at the site of
Kenchreae, the ancient Aegean harbour for Corinth, last
year's American excavations revealed constructions from
imperial Roman times that are at present under six to ten
feet of water.

On the east coast of Attica there are cuttings in the bed-
rock for waggon wheels in the classical Greek manner for
roadways, leading down to the sea and continuing for
some distance beneath the water. Here certainly the land
has not sunk, but the sea has risen.

(Similar wheel tracks beneath the sea have been reported for the island of Malta; but there, for lack of any
chronological setting—though it would be my guess that
the tracks were cut in Hellenistic or Roman times—the
evident fact that the sea has risen since the tracks were cut
is not very helpful.)

Recent American excavation of a Bronze Age settlement on the Aegean island of Keos has disclosed traces of
an ancient fortification wall running beneath the present
sea level to a depth of more than two metres. Since the
wall is assigned to the Middle Helladic period, it is clear

that there was less water in the Mediterranean around 1500 B.C. than there is today. This would be proof of a cooler phase of the general planetary climate at that time. Whether or not there was accompanying heavier rainfall cannot be inferred.

Along the southern coast of Turkey in the stretch corresponding to ancient Cilicia, a colleague of mine reports that numerous foundations of buildings are visible beneath the sea—structures that must once have been based on dry land.

As far as I can judge from these varied and widespread cases, the rise in the Mediterranean (and hence also in the planetary ocean level) since shortly before and after the birth of Christ is uniformly measurable at about ten feet. Such a difference in the Mediterranean Sea may not seem a very significant event until one tries to calculate the enormous mass of water from melted ice that must have entered the oceans of the world to effect such a rise. I should not care to venture any estimate of the number of added degrees Fahrenheit in the earth's atmospheric temperature that might be involved in the melting process; but I gather that is it not as large as one might hastily assume. Nevertheless, the climatic repercussions in terms of continental storm tracks and zonal weather patterns could have been quite disproportionately accentuated.

But while it is thus a comparatively simple matter to show by the discrepancy in the sea level that a colder (and therefore also wetter?) climate prevailed in the Mediterranean during the classical period, it is much more difficult to adduce evidence that the contrary condition of increased warmth accompanied by scantier rainfall dominated the preceding Late Mycenaean period. There is a considerable body of evidence indicative of such a climatic phase at the end of Roman imperial times; but for the earlier period of the late second millennium before Christ the traces of high water in the Mediterranean have been obliterated or are no longer legible. For lack of such evidence we must look for another way of attacking the problem. That such a way exists, I shall try to show in my next lecture.

2

MINOANS, MYCENAEANS, AND DORIANS

I have had little success in persuading my classical colleagues that the natural catastrophe which overwhelmed the Aegean island of Santorin, in antiquity known as Thera, was of such magnitude as to have altered the entire course of human history in the lands surrounding the Aegean. Although the authoritative Austrian publication of ancient Thera paid due attention to the destruction that had devastated the island in pre-classical time and drew suggestive comparison with the great eruption of Krakatoa in the Sunda Strait between Sumatra and Java in 1883, ancient historians and archaeologists gave no thought to the inevitable human misfortune attendant on so tremendous an event. Their neglect may partly have been due to an unconscious rejection of any item that could not be fitted into their reconstruction of the past because no even approximate date for its occurrence could be ascertained. But I am rather inclined to think that the whole episode struck them as too sensational to be given any place in their professionally restrained and scientifically meticulous dealings with the past.

However, there has been a somewhat more receptive reaction during the present decade. In particular Professor Spyridon Marinatos has not shied from elevating Santorin to a factor of major moment in reconstructing the archaeological history of Minoan Crete.

Discontinuity in Greek Civilization

I have visited Santorin a number of times; but my first glimpse of it more than fifty years ago remains unforgettable. The small Greek steamer on which I was returning to Athens from Crete put into the ghostly harbour of Santorin near midnight under a full moon riding high. The seventy-mile crossing from Crete had been rough; but all motion ceased as we slid under the shelter of the thousand-foot walls of shadow-black volcanic rock that lined the broad harbour. I noticed that we were moored to a floating barrel-buoy hitched to the quay, 'We cannot anchor,' said the ship's mate, 'the sea here has no bottom.' From the landing place a paved pathway led up in steep zigzags to a silver-white town on the skyline. Down this ladder-like descent there moved in and out of the moonlight a scattering of men and donkeys, stirred into sleepy animation by our arrival. Everything was weirdly unreal. 'What freak of nature', I asked myself, 'created this astonishing place?'

Until rather recently I had always supposed that the huge semi-landlocked sea basin of Santorin was the crater of a volcano that had blown its top when the sea infiltrated it and the superheated steam thus generated had exploded the cone. But it appears that this is not the correct explanation. What must actually have happened was far more terrific.

Judging by what happened at Krakatoa, the final disaster on Santorin must have been preceded by a considerable period of severe eruption of the volcano that once occupied the north-west corner of the island. The discharge must have been sufficiently intense and prolonged to have heaped up the enormous layer of volcanic ash and pumice that still covers the island and has in places a depth of 100 feet. As at Krakatoa (where the preliminary ejection of ash lasted more than three months) there was no great outflow of lava, but rather a continuous emptying of the underground store of volcanic slack in the form of dust and papillae.

On 27 August 1883 the entire superstructure of the Krakatoa volcano collapsed into the great void that had been hollowed out beneath it to a depth of some 1,500 feet below sea level. Into this abyss, now left open to the sea, a gigantic inrush of ocean water caused a consequent rebounding outrush of tidal waves, some of which are said to have been over 100 feet high. A Dutch warship in nearby waters was left stranded half a mile inland. Thirty-six thousand lives were lost and nearly three hundred native villages were destroyed. The uproar at one point was so terrific that the sound of it was distinctly audible in western Australia 2,000 miles away! Surrounding districts of Java and Sumatra were plunged into a total darkness that lasted several days. In the upper atmosphere the finer dust of the eruption drifted several times around the earth and lingered aloft for many months, as was evident from that year's magnificent sunsets seen in many countries.

Inasmuch as the sea-filled cauldron of Santorin measures twice the diameter and consequently has four times the superficial area of the cauldron created by Krakatoa, with much the same depth, the disaster that overwhelmed ancient Thera must have been of much greater intensity. No living thing could possibly have survived on the island; and nearby Crete (no portion of which was more than 140 miles distant) must have been wrapped in darkness of falling ash amid terrifying storms of wind and rain.

Who is not reminded of the vivid description of the destruction of the island of Atlantis as recounted to Solon by the Egyptian priest in Plato's *Timaeus*, how there were tremendous earthquakes and inundations and in a single ensuing terrible day and night the island sank into the sea and disappeared? Since the priest, according to Kritias' account, asserted that 'whenever anything great or glorious or *otherwise noteworthy* occurs, it is written down and preserved in our temples', and since Egypt, less than 500 miles distant from Santorin in direct air line and regularly visited by Minoan and Mycenaean traders and emissaries, could not conceivably have failed to have knowledge of the great disaster in the Aegean, is it not entirely reasonable to interpret Santorin as the ultimate origin of the legend of Atlantis?

I am of course aware that, as F. M. Cornford remarked in his edition of Plato's *Timaeus*, 'serious scholars now agree that Atlantis probably owed its existence entirely to Plato's imagination'; but these scholars have neglected to consider Santorin and have been distracted by Plato's embellishments of the original account. Like the Homeric Troy inflated too large for tiny Hissarlik, Atlantis grew in Plato's thoughts into a continent too large for the Mediterranean and was in consequence exiled to the greater ocean beyond Gibraltar Strait—a region of which the old Egyptian recorders had never heard.

Nor should they have disregarded that Plato's tale of Atlantis differs from the normal type of his myths in that it is specifically distinguished as derived from genuine oral family tradition, 'although passing strange, nevertheless entirely true, even as wise Solon once asserted'. Calculation will show its chronological frame to be historically sound—at least, if we assume for Kritias' great-grandfather Dropides that his relationship with Solon (as perhaps hinted in the remark that Solon had addressed many of his verses to him) was that of an elderly admirer to an adolescent youth. That Solon had visited Egypt and sojourned there long enough to establish intelligent communication with the Saite priesthood, will hardly be challenged.

A remarkable detail that should convince the most sceptical of the genuineness of Solon's conversation with the Saite priest is the latter's unambiguous statement that the older Greek race had been reduced to an unlettered and uncivilized remnant which, like children, had to learn its letters anew. This claim we now know to be entirely exact; but we have no reason to believe that Plato himself was aware of it.

I am accordingly prepared to maintain that in Solon's day there was preserved in Egyptian temple chronicles the mention of an island that had sunk beneath the sea during a tremendous natural upheaval, and that this island—for which Plato invented the name Atlantis—was no other than Santorin.

Until the pre-classical remains lying buried beneath the thick mantle of volcanic ash on Santorin have been adequately investigated, we shall have no certain guide to tell us the date of the disaster. About a generation ago a tentative sounding by two members of the French School at Athens retrieved some fragments of plaster fresco painting and vases of local manufacture that were classed with advanced Late Minoan I, suggesting that the eruption could not have occurred much earlier than the close of the fifteenth century B.C. Only last year an American expedition investigating a pre-classical site on the island of Keos in the Aegean, 120 miles north-west of Santorin, found indubitable evidence that a Middle Helladic settlement had been totally ruined by earthquake about the end of the fifteenth century B.C. The chronological agreement with the supposed date of the Theran disaster is too close to rule out the probability that it was the volcanic cataclysm on Thera that occasioned the Kean destruction by earthquake. Presumably, the many times greater island of Crete, situated as close to Thera as Keos is, did not escape comparable calamity. There too—as everyone now knows—the traces of destruction by earthquake are clearly seen in the excavated palace sites, such as Knossos and Malliá and Kato Zakro. There is an increasing inclination in archaeological circles to equate their destruction with that of Thera. Certainly the loss of life and material damage must have been tremendous throughout the Aegean basin. But though it would be difficult to exaggerate the scope and magnitude of this disaster, without parallel in all Mediterranean history, it would be unwarranted to infer that the Minoan civilization was so overwhelmed by calamity that it could not recover itself or continue its former ways of life. As the recent war has demonstrated to us of today, nations survive the destruction of their cities along with the annihilation of a sizeable percentage of their population and, in the course of a single generation or two, restore themselves to their previous cultural conditions of material prosperity. So it should have been in Minoan antiquity, had not other intrusive factors intervened.

One such intrusive factor—a very calamitous one for the Minoan power—was the aggressive might of mainland Greece, which seems to have seized the opportunity of the disruption incident on the disaster of Santorin to invade the Cretan isle and establish itself in control at Knossos. In whatever sense this still unclear chapter in Minoan history may ultimately be written out by the archaeologists and cultural historians, one fact emerges with sufficient clarity from the chronologic haze still hanging over the ancient Aegean. The occurrence of archaeological material with Late Minoan connexions beneath the volcanic debris on Santorin, coupled with the entire absence of any reported traces from the heyday of Mycenaean prosperity anywhere on the island, combines to exculpate Santorin from having contributed to the decline of Mycenaean civilization, since this decline belongs to a period at least a couple of centuries after the great eruption. We must therefore search for some wholly different explanation for the disintegration of the Greek Mycenaean civilization.

This conclusion conforms very closely to the dictum of the old Egyptian priest as reported in the *Timaeus,* wherein he distinguished three separate events—the submergence of the Atlantid island, the defeat of the Atlantid armies by the bravery of the ancestral Athenians, and the destruction of the older civilization by the sun's departure from its wonted courses. Since the first two of this triad seem to have a firm basis in historic fact, it is only reasonable to consider whether we may give credence also to the third.

In the absence of any other ancient account dealing with the issue, we shall have to turn to modern archaeological investigation for a clue to the cultural retrogression of Greece at the close of the Mycenaean period. But here we encounter an initial difficulty. As everyone knows—or ought to know—the inherent character of archaeological data is that they are essentially, and oftentimes exclusively, self-contained within their own material limits. As such, they are not automatically or necessarily convertible into historical fact, least of all into political events.

Notwithstanding this objection, if we are to make any headway at this point we shall have to examine the archaeological evidence and scrutinize it sufficiently closely to derive any useful understanding of the aid that it may offer. I need not apologize for its professional nature or its intricacy of detail. There is no royal road cut straight across its detours and bypaths. If its material construction is of clay, this is because clay from the potter's oven is the one truly indestructible substance in human employ. All else rots or rusts or otherwise disappears: oven-baked clay endures. To be sure, it is easily broken and freely discarded; but it survives all the more obstinately, since the more it is divided, the more there is of it. I am forcibly reminded of the delightful ballad of the Sorcerer's Apprentice.

As Mycenaean ceramics are currently classified, material from the period of greatest cultural prosperity is known as Late Helladic III A. It dates roughly to the fourteenth century B.C. The ensuing phase of scarcely slackened cultural activity and power in the thirteenth century is classed as Late Helladic III B. This period was rudely shaken by the destruction of the great palaces at Mycenae, Tiryns, and Pylos, an event for which the year 1230 B.C. has become a sort of chronological rallying point in the reconstruction of Mycenaean political history. Late Helladic III B is succeeded by a phase of marked and rather rapid decline, distinguished, as might be anticipated—we are not a very imaginative profession!—as III C and identified with the span of years from *c.* 1230 to the close of the ensuing century. As Professor Blegen notes, for general purposes III A may be equated with the fourteenth, III B with the thirteenth, and III C with the twelfth century. In the present state of knowledge one can hardly be more precise.

It will be our problem, if we seek to explain the pathology of cultural decadence in the ancient Mediterranean, to discover (if we can) some cause for the sharp decline in the Mycenaean culture during the third period and the virtual extinction of that culture thereafter. For, to speak of a fourth Mycenaean phase for the eleventh century (let us say, a III D!) would be to ascribe flesh and blood to a shadow or a ghost. By the turn of the millennium at 1000 B.C. Mycenaean civilization had virtually ceased to exist. Yet there was not yet discernible any classical civilization, either. Between the two there is a gap of emptiness wide enough to engulf any bridge that you might try to build from the pre-Hellenic to the Hellenic world.

I shall speak, therefore, of a Mycenaean cultural decline equivalent to a virtual annihilation of all higher civilization; but I shall not admit the easy but specious acceptance of this as due to that stage of natural senility which, in Spengler's and (somewhat more disguised) in Toynbee's biological fallacy, engenders a material and spiritual debility that no geriatric manipulation can cure. If we are dissatisfied—as I think we should be—at resolving the problem of Mycenaean decadence in terms of a metaphor from the life-cycle of animal existence, we must seek among more materialistic causes for an acceptable theory. The one to which the majority of present-day scholars is most especially partial is the so-called Dorian invasion, to which they attribute the entire calamity of the destruction of Mycenaean sites and the wane of Mycenaean prosperity and power. Their argument runs that some sort of violently hostile invasion could alone have been responsible for so much irreparable damage, and since Greek historical tradition records no other newcomers into Greece between Mycenaean and classical times, *ergo* it is the Dorians who must have destroyed the Mycenaean realm.

Before demonstrating the outright impossibility of making the Dorians responsible for the collapse of Mycenaean civilization, it is essential that we should have some sort of reliable and coherent picture of the material conditions obtaining in southern Greece toward the close of the Mycenaean age. Such a picture can most readily be supplied by excerpting from an authoritative work published only this last year and devoted to the very subject of the end of the Mycenaean age. It is entitled *The Last Mycenaeans and their Successors*, and its author is Vincent Desborough.

Here, then, with only occasional intrusive comments of my own, is Desborough's account:

The history of the last quarter of the thirteenth century can possibly be reconstructed as follows. The first sign of trouble is visible in an attack on Mycenae itself; it does not seem that the attackers penetrated within the citadel; but considerable damage was done to imposing buildings immediately adjoining. There is no proof that other sites suffered destruction at this time, nor do we know the cause of the attack. The shock must have been considerable, but was not catastrophic.

Fairly soon afterwards, however, a really serious invasion [of the Peloponnese] took place, the effects of which are visible in destruction of sites, in their desertion, and in a movement of population. Many sites were abandoned without our knowing whether there was destruction as well.

Here I might comment that a less tendentious way to put this would be to say that these sites were deserted without any trace of destruction or conflagration! Among the abandoned settlements were

two important sites in the Argolid as well as some minor settlements, and probably a considerable number of sites in Laconia and the southwest Peloponnese. As a result of this destruction and desertion there was a movement of population to less dangerous [why less dangerous?] and, in some cases, originally less populous sites. Achaea in the northwest Peloponnese and the island of Kephallenia are examples of areas where a considerable increase of population is to be observed. The east coast of Attica now becomes more fashionable than previously, and it is fairly clear that a sizeable body of refugees made their way to Cyprus and to Tarsus in Cilicia. Of these movements we can speak with some confidence; other groups may have gone elsewhere.

The details just rehearsed may be somewhat uncomfortably complex for remembering; but they are all extremely significant, as I intend to show. Meanwhile I continue with Desborough:

The route followed by the invaders and their geographical origin obviously need careful attention, as well as the further effects of their destructiveness on the Mycenaean world ... The direction and route of this major invasion may be considered in the light of the areas which were affected and in the light of the direction taken by refugees from the regions which suffered disaster.

With admirable reasoning Desborough proceeds to show that the attack could not have been organized from within Mycenaean territory. It must therefore have penetrated from outside Greece. But, as Desborough proceeds to argue, there was no racial group to organize such an invasion and no available route by which they might have come, since all the possible routes of entry seem blocked by the archaeological evidence of Mycenaean culture surviving in the very regions through which the invader would have had to pass. In the first place, if the invaders came by sea, says Desborough,

it does not seem possible that they came from the eastern Mediterranean, as they would have had to pass through the South Aegean, which remained unharmed. Also, it is hardly likely that they came down the Adriatic or from South Italy or Sicily, since there would not then have been a movement of refugees to Kephallenia, in the precise direction from which the invaders would have come.

For similar reasons, a seaborne invasion from the northeast Aegean is ruled out; so that the only logical conclusion must be that the invasion did not come by sea.

Minoans, Mycenaeans, and Dorians

Desborough continues:

The hypothesis of a land invasion has two merits . . . However, it raises the problem of the invaders' eventual settlement . . . They might of course have occupied all the areas through which they passed, but there are good reasons for rejecting this idea . . . First, it must be stressed that there is no single object or custom which can be associated with the invaders in any region passed through by them.

Secondly, there is evidence of considerable depopulation in Laconia and Messenia and

in the great majority of cases archaeological excavation or survey shows that the abandonment of sites . . . was an absolute one. That is to say, there was no further occupation of the sites by anyone—at least not until considerably later. This is not a matter of a few sites only; the number that has now been identified is very considerable. Not only have we no evidence of any alien objects, we have no evidence of any settlement at all. The natural and logical answer is that the invaders did not settle in any of the areas which they overran, but departed.

I submit that a better inference would be that *there were no invaders*.

Consider the evidence once again. No plausible route of entry for the invaders can be suggested. They did not come by sea, for reasons already cited. They did not come by land because, along the eastern shore, Attica and the Argolid were not occupied by an invader at this time, and along the western shore of Greece, Achaia became an area of refuge for the native Peloponnesians, especially on and around the Panachaic mountain slope behind Patras, with a preference for the western coastal area

(Desborough, p. 227), directly in the path of the invader, who apparently left them undisturbed without any trace of his passage through their territory. Yet, at this period between 1200 and 1150, according to Desborough, 'Laconia and Messenia, these previously flourishing districts, were now almost denuded of their inhabitants'. Still, there is no trace of any foreign element replacing the fugitives. On the contrary, what survived of the Mycenaean world continued with culture and customs unchanged, albeit with considerable indication of degeneration. In the Argolid, especially at Mycenae, 'there was some attempt at recovery'; while other sites that had not been abandoned continued to be 'inhabited by Mycenaeans and not by invaders'. To quote Desborough once more,

There is no trace of destruction elsewhere [than at Mycenae] at this time [*sc. c.* 1150 B.C.], and the evidence of such sites as Argos and Asine shows that the inhabitants continued the Mycenaean way of life for a while. There is no sign of any intrusive element, and indeed the cause of the disaster at Mycenae [*sc.* the destruction of the 'Granary' by fire] has not been established.

All in all, an extraordinary and paradoxical situation, in which there is no sign of the presence of any hostile invader, for whom no route of entry and passage can be found; yet the native population is deserting its established habitations as though driven by some invisible and nameless terror, 'like ghosts from an enchanter fleeing'.

In all this complexity one thing at least is entirely certain: even if there really was some sort of invasion from the outside world into southern Greece during the opening decades of the thirteenth century, the invaders could not possibly have been the Dorians, for the simple and sufficient reason that when the Dorians did come, they came to stay—as their dialect, widespread over most of the Peloponnese, coupled with the testimony of the ancient historians, unambiguously certifies. But Desborough's hypothetical and elusive invaders did *not* remain. Therefore it could not have been the Dorians that invaded Greece in late Mycenaean times, driving the inhabitants to flight and then themselves disappearing utterly, as though dissolving into thin air to leave not a rack behind.

What actually happened in late Mycenaean history was not an invasion from outside, but an evacuation from within; not an enemy incursion, but a dispersal—a *diaspora*—of the Mycenaean inhabitants of the Peloponnese. I have already remarked their arrival on the western shoreland of Achaia and the western slopes of the Panachaic mountain, as well as their migration to Kephallenia (and perhaps to others of the Ionian island group off Greece's western coast). The evidence for this will be found in Per Ålin's recent monograph entitled *das Ende der mykenischen Fundstätten auf dem griechischen Festland,* in which you will find statistics on the incidence of Mycenaean pottery from all three periods of Late Helladic—that is, III A, III B, and III C.

It is not only the comparative paucity of this last class of pottery ware, III C, assignable to the twelfth century and suggestive of a considerable cultural recession, that emerges from Ålin's tabulations, but equally clearly and emphatically the persistence of this late ware in certain districts contemporaneously with its virtual disappearance elsewhere, and not only its continued occurrence in these special regions but its actual increase, to suggest a flourishing community at the very time that other parts of the Peloponnese were being abandoned. Thus, to be specific, pottery sherds from the twelfth century are very scant in central Greece (Boeotia, Euboea and Phokis) and even more so in Laconia and Messenia (where most modern exploration has been done), whereas they continue strong in Attica and even become abundant in western Achaea. Ålin's survey of the Greek mainland should be supplemented by remarking, as Professor Blegen among others has done, that 'in the Ionian islands toward the west, and in the east, especially in Rhodes and Cyprus and beyond in Asia Minor and along the Syrian and Palestinian coast, pottery of the Mycenaean III C style, or related to it, appears in some quantity, suggesting that the latest Mycenaean culture, or contacts with it, were still maintained in these regions'. In other words, there has been a Mycenaean migration westward and eastward from the Greek mainland.

The island of Cyprus, in particular, deserves closer scrutiny, because here there are indications of destruction around the year 1200 B.C., suggesting local resistance to invasion; but since the rebuilt towns and settlements have yielded Late Mycenaean ware of Argive type, it is well-nigh obligatory to conclude that the invaders were Mycenaean Greeks from the Peloponnese and that the disturbance on Cyprus was due to an influx of kinsmen from the mainland—in short, an element in what I am calling the Mycenaean *diaspora*.

But it was not alone mainland Greece and Cyprus that witnessed migratory movements of population toward the turn of the thirteenth to the twelfth century. In the year 1227—or just about the time that current opinion assigns to the burning of the palaces at Mycenae, Tiryns and Pylos—Libyan tribes from the Cyrenaica, accompanied by various foreign people referred to as 'northerners from all lands', invaded the Nile delta, but were defeated by the Egyptians. An even more dangerous incursion from a different quarter threatened Egypt thirty years later. This too was repulsed, in the sea and land battle described in grandiloquent phrases in the often quoted inscription of Rameses III at Medînet Habu:

The isles were restless, disturbed among themselves. No land stood before their weapons, from Khatti, Qode, Carchemish, Arzawa and Alishiya on. They pitched their camps in Amurru; they desolated its peoples, and its land was like that which never has been. They came with fire before them, onward toward Egypt. Their main might was the Pelest, the Tjekeri, Shekelesh, Daanau, Uashasha. These were united and set their hands upon the land unto the Circle of the Earth . . . Those who reached my frontier, their seed is not; their heart and their soul are perished for ever. Those who had assembled ahead of them by sea, the full flame was in their front before the harbour mouths; a wall of metal surrounded them on the shore. They were dragged, capsized, and laid low upon the strand; slain and made into heaps from stern to bow of their ships. Their possessions were cast upon the water.

From the pharaoh's point of view, 'it was a famous victory!'

'The isles were restless.' What isles? One naturally thinks of the island-studded Aegean, since otherwise (except for Cyprus) there are no available candidates in the eastern Mediterranean. But, for 1196 B.C.—which falls at approximately the beginning of Mycenaean IIIC—the Aegean islands offer no archaeological indication of unrest or disturbance. As Desborough remarks for this period, there is 'no evidence of destruction in the islands of the central and south Aegean, especially the Dodecanese'; and apropos of Rhodes he adds that 'it is reasonably certain that no disturbance marked the transition from IIIB to IIIC and that there was no lessening of prosperity in C'. An identical situation obtained in nearby Kos and Kalymnos where (according to Desborough) we may 'say that there are positive signs that there was no destruction' at the close of the thirteenth century. And yet 'the isles were restless, disturbed among themselves'. Or is this what Rameses asserted? I have only a bare smattering of hieroglyphic learning; but I think that I am correct in asserting that, precisely because there were virtually no islands in Egypt, there was no specific ancient Egyptian word for such a feature. The hieroglyphic sign often rendered in translation as 'island' properly denotes a sandy tract or shore, and is widely used as a determinative symbol for foreign lands or regions beyond the Nile valley. Hence to write that 'the isles were restless' is to mistranslate the hieroglyphic text: it would be more correct to write 'the foreign lands' (or perhaps 'the shorelands'), especially as the places specifically named, in so far as they can be geographically identified, all belong to the Syrian frontier zone, where the 'Circle of the Earth' presumably is also to be located. The Aegean world thus drops from the scene.

So likewise do the other distant lands which some historians have conjured up out of the vowelless hieroglyphic recording of the names of the various participants in the two invasions. By playing a sort of philological game of hopscotch with the consonantal skeletons of these names they have connected the Tjeker with Zakro in Crete, the Daanu with the Danaoi of the Homeric epic, the Shekelesh with the Sicels, the Shardana with Sardinia, and the Tursha with the Etruscans, thereby conflating out of precarious guesswork a Mediterranean-wide *Völkerwanderung* of formidable proportions, where all that actually reached Egypt was a motley group of minor residents of the southern Anatolian and Syrian shoreland. Judging by the survival of their tribal names in similar-sounding place-names (and remembering that the correct vocalization of the hieroglyphic words is unknown), the Shekel-sha may be the people of Askalon, the Tursha may have taken their name from Dor, where the Tjeker are known to have settled. As everyone agrees, the Peleset are the folk of Palestine. True, the Luka should be Lycians, and the Akaiwash may perfectly well have been Achaeans; but these last might equally well have been Achaeans from Cyprus or Cilicia rather than from Mycenaean Argos in Greece. As H. R. Hall pointed out long ago in his still authoritative *Ancient History of the Near East*, 'Shardana and Shakalsha are already found hovering on the Asiatic coasts and taking service in the wars of Palestine as early as the time of the Tell el-Amarna letters (*c.* 1370 B.C.)' and 'Danuna appear at the same time on the coast of Palestine', and, since Hall's last edition, have turned up also at Kara Tepe in North

Syria. These three, therefore, are longstanding dwellers in the eastern Mediterranean, not foreigners breaking in from afar. There is no evidence of any great dislocation of tribes out of the forest lands of Europe or the steppe lands of Asia. Yet something has been compelling the folk of southern Anatolia to abandon their accustomed places of abode. The Hittites of the Anatolian plateau beyond the Taurus mountain chain might somehow have been involved, since they too were moved to evacuate their homeland at this time. Certainly, the pressure could not have been the other way about: even if they combined their forces, these miscellaneous coastal tribes would not have had strength to destroy the great Hittite empire. Nonetheless, at just this period of the raids against Egypt—which is to say, close on the year 1200 B.C.— Hittite Shubbililiuma's empire ended after two centuries of power and disappeared from the stage of history.

Who, or what, destroyed the Hittite power? Seemingly, no human agency, since archaeology has discovered no one to whom the role of destruction can be assigned. Like the Mycenaeans in the Peloponnese at this same period, the Hittites abandoned their towns and villages in the heart of Asia Minor. We know whither they migrated, inasmuch as they survived in greatly enfeebled state in northern Syria below the Taurus mountain rampart, to be bearers of the 'sub-Hittite' culture in the early centuries of the first millennium B.C. Why did they migrate? Written history offers only one hint—a great famine.

In this connexion it is pertinent to point out that there were further migrations in mainland Greece in addition to those previously reviewed. In the nineteenth book of his *History*, Diodorus Siculus reports that the Boeotians were obliged to retire into Thessaly at the time of the Trojan War and did not find their way back to Boeotia until the fourth generation. Whatever date we may suppose to be intended by this reference to Troy, the Boeotian return to their previously abandoned country should have occurred about the year 1000 B.C. (give or take a quarter of a century) and their previous departure into voluntary exile would coincide—as far as can at present be ascertained—with the burning and permanent abandonment of the palace on the Copaic island hill of Gla.

About another, roughly contemporaneous, Greek migration into northern Greece ancient tradition has considerably more to say. It was the forerunner of that Dorian influx into the Peloponnese of which I have already spoken under its fictitious modern name. It is true that there are occasional ancient references to this event as a military operation—Plato in the *Laws* speaks of the Dorians as an army (στράτευμα) and Pausanias twice speaks of them as an expeditionary force (στόλος)—but the overwhelming consensus of ancient authors (Pausanias included) favours a different and very significant appellation. For them the 'Dorian invasion' of our modern historians was the *Return of the Heraklids* to their ancestral land. The Greek word for this return was that universally used for an exile's return to the land he was forced to leave— κάθοδος.

The Heraklids (which is to say, professed linear descendants or tribal followers of the legendary hero-god Herakles) had presumably been inhabiting Argos; but however we identify them, ancient tradition emphatically asserted that they departed from the Peloponnese, betook themselves by way of Attica to northern Greece, whence after a considerable lapse of time (a hundred years according to one account) they made their way back once more into the Peloponnese—not *in propria persona*, since the original emigrants were by this time dead, but in their third or fourth generation. They brought with them a mixed company of Doric-speaking people, with whom they had become associated during their term of absence from their motherland.

If I am right in assuming that it was from Argos and the Argolid that the Heraklid migration originated, archaeological evidence of their departure may be sought in the widespread abandonment of Argive sites in Mycenaean III C, i.e. in the late thirteenth or early twelfth century. At any rate, in order for the Heraklids to have returned to Greece it is obvious that they had first to quit that country; and the only archaeological indication that fits their setting forth belongs to Late Helladic III C.

The story of this Heraklid movement is rather involved. In so far as it can be pieced together from classical Greek accounts, it runs briefly as follows:

Setting out from Argos, the Heraklid band attempted to settle on or near the gulf of Corinth, but were forced to desist by the opposition of the occupants of that region. The Heraklid leader—traditionally Hyllos, Herakles' own son, though this seems logically and chronologically meaningless—was slain in single combat; after which the self-made exiles moved out of the Peloponnese to find shelter in Attica. There some of them remained near Marathon, while the remainder continued northward into

Thessaly. There we lose sight of them for a considerable time, unless we may infer that some of their leaders attained to positions of authority in Thessaly and Macedon; for in the classical age the princely family of the Thessalian Aleuadai and the ruling dynasty of Macedon both claimed descent from Herakles. (It will be recalled that Alexander the Great insisted that Herakles was his ultimate ancestor.) Tradition held that it was a full century after their departure from the Peloponnese that the Heraklids made their return. One group, at least, must have been living among the Doric-speaking tribes of Epirus and the Pindus range. Being now in their third generation, they had associated so closely with their rude farmer-shepherd hosts that they had exchanged their own Achaean or Arcadian speech in favour of the Doric variant of Greek. My own country affords abundant examples of such loss of the language of their country of origin by immigrants in their third generation of residence. Even so, we do not know (and cannot know) whether the Heraklids themselves spoke Doric Greek at the time of their return to Greece. A familiar anecdote in Herodotus tells us that the Heraklids, even in later time, were conscious that they were not Dorians despite that they were Spartan kings!

In the course of their migration moving south through Aetolia, the Heraklids and their Dorian followers reached the western end of the Corinthian gulf. Here, it is reported, they were delayed by famine before crossing the narrow strait that separates Central Greece from the Peloponnese. Continuing southward into Elis, they relinquished this latter territory to the Aetolians who had led them across into Achaia, and proceeded, apparently without encountering opposition, up the open valley of the Alpheios. From its headwaters some of their company crossed the low watershed westward into the fertile Messenian basin, while the rest followed the easy descent down the valley of the Eurotas to Sparta. The rivers with their life-giving water had guided them.

The course that I have suggested for the Dorian advance into the Peloponnese agrees with that taken by the Franks in their penetration of the Morea in the thirteenth century of our era, if we may judge from the line of their castles still to be seen at Glarentza in Elis and at Karýtaena on the upper Alpheios, and their occupation of Mistrá above the Eurotas and of Monemvasía on the Laconian coast. I believe that this was likewise the route of penetration by the Slavs when they moved down the west coast of Greece from Epirus into the Peloponnese during the seventh and eighth centuries after Christ.

The Frankish seizure of the Peloponnese was achieved by force of armed might; but there is no evidence that the Heraklids' return to their ancestral land in company with the Doric tribes was anything more violent than an unopposed occupation of a depopulated countryside. It is true that Pausanias preserves a tradition that the descendants of Pylian Nestor were driven from their home by the Heraklids and sought refuge in Athens; but Pausanias adds, immediately after, that 'there was no expulsion of the ancient Messenians by the Dorians', but a sharing of the land with them under a Heraklid as king. This ruler took up his residence not at the palace site of Pylos (which seems never to have been reoccupied) but at Stenyklāros in the upper Messenian plain, where a low ridge of hills divides Messenia from the headwaters of the Alpheios. Equally significant is the ceramic evidence from most of the Messenian sites that there was a break in continuity between the latest Mycenaean and the earliest classical period. Most of the Mycenaean settlements that were abandoned in the twelfth century were not chosen for reoccupation by the Dorians. The intervening lapse of three generations and a full hundred years of time had obliterated old memories and the physical traces of previous human existence. These changes of abode, which archaeological reconnaissance has established on un-arguable evidence, constitute a material proof of his-torical discontinuity between the two cultural epochs.

If you ask what part in this phenomenon of cleavage between the Mycenaean and the classic phase of Hellenic civilization was played by the destruction of the Mycen-aean palaces, I must reply that an answer to this question cannot be elicited by archaeological investigation, which (having only tri-millennially old traces of combustion to work from) cannot possibly point a finger at the doers of the deed or their motives, or even say whether or not the catastrophes were deliberately occasioned. Conflagration may be due to human carelessness, to stroke of lightning, to arson as a result of internal intrigue as well as of civil rebellion. As yet, it is not even possible to say that Mycenae, Tiryns, and Pylos suffered destruction simul-taneously or within the same decade or even within the same generation. This is a point brought out by the Swedish scholar Per Ålin, to whose statistical study of the incidence of Late Mycenaean pottery on the 390 sites of mainland Greece where such pottery has so far been found, I am indebted for the following comment, which I translate to read,

We are naturally inclined to picture the course of events at Mycenae and Tiryns as though simultaneously at both places the lower towns and the acropoleis went up in flames, while elsewhere in Greece these catastrophes were echoed by similar conflagrations. But the actual situation is considerably more complex; so that at present we are entitled only to speak of events as engendering widespread destruction by fire and abandonment of sites during the final phase of LH III B,

which is to say, the latter decades of the thirteenth century B.C.

None the less I am inclined to the view that the evidence favours the destruction and abandonment of the Mycenaean palaces during a fairly limited period of time, but not necessarily simultaneously or by common counsel or design.

In my concluding lecture I shall suggest what might have brought on a widespread sacking and burning of the ruling centres, confining myself for the moment to the pregnant remark that the Linear B tablets uncovered at Pylos indicate that the local ruler was intensively engaged in collecting and storing the edible yield of the district under his control.

And here it might be well to pause and review the situation that I have been attempting to describe. Briefly stated, I have been seeking to establish two quite simple propositions, namely, that the Dorians had nothing whatever to do with the collapse of Mycenaean civilization, since they did not enter the Peloponnese until long after that collapse had already taken place; and secondly, that the political and cultural disintegration of the Mycenaean age is to be understood as having been due, not to destruction at the violent hands of outsiders, but as engendered from within by local conditions that compelled the abandonment of most of the smaller communities and instigated a sacking of the palaces of the ruling caste, with the result that a hitherto prosperous countryside was left virtually unoccupied, to remain at the lowest endurable subsistence level for the better part of two centuries.

This is the picture that seems to be implied by the archaeological investigations pursued with ever-increasing scope in recent decades. Even so, it is a picture that must strike many as thoroughly implausible. It is implausible because it fails to supply any reason why the Mycenaean inhabitants of mainland Greece should have thus abandoned their homes and migrated—west, north, and east—to seek refuge elsewhere. I must leave to my next and final lecture the reason that I think is sound and valid, although I suspect that you already know what it is that I am going to say, since the old Egyptian priest of Plato's *Timaeus* put his finger on it, ages ago.

3

THE KEY TO THE RIDDLE

In the preceding lecture, when I sought to establish the (to me wholly evident) fact that the Dorians had no part or share in the destruction of Mycenaean civilization, I had no intention of denying the historical actuality of the Dorian occupation of the Peloponnese or of minimizing their contribution to the racial composition of classical Greece. Quite the contrary! The return of the Heraklids to their parental land, after two or three generations of self-imposed exile, as leaders and rulers of various tribal aggregations of Doric-speaking north-west Greeks—taken along with the traditions of an Ionian migration to the western coasts and shoreland islands of Asia Minor—is virtually our only source of light on the otherwise totally obscure period between the dissolution of the Mycenaean kingdoms and the reconstruction of a wholly new phase of Hellenic civilization.

Let me revert, therefore, to the Heraklid return to the territory that was formerly Mycenaean Greece.

Ancient tradition records their arrival only by way of Aetolia and the western mouth of the Corinthian gulf to Elis and thence into Messenia. But I think that we are bound by the archaeological evidence and the ancient tradition of the partition of the Peloponnese under rival Heraklid rulers to postulate a second stream of Heraklid return, reaching the Peloponnese by sea and landing on its eastern coast at Argos.

Reference to such a sea passage by returning Heraklids may be detected in the classical tradition that a certain piece of rocky ground close to the shore, about midway between Tiryns and Argos, was known as the 'Tēmenion' because it was there that Tēmenos, the Heraklid king of Doric Argos, had landed. A single place-name is not enough to build history on. But there is archaeological evidence to supplement it. Desborough claims that after the destruction of the palaces at Mycenae and Tiryns an 'apparently undisturbed survival of the Mycenaeans in the Argolid perhaps lasted nearly three generations' (which, if correct, would bring the date down to about 1100 B.C.). At some time thereafter—though Desborough does not set a specific date—he asserts that there is evidence for an arrival of people of non-Mycenaean orientation moving (as he puts it) 'peacefully into a depressed and depopulated area'. These un-Mycenaean people can only have been the Dorians, since the Argolid became a Doric-speaking land and no other intruders than the Dorians are recorded or indicated.

We are obliged, therefore, to set this portion of the return of the Heraklids at least as late as the eleventh century. In this connexion it should be noted that these newcomers practised cist burials and that their stone-lined graves were often dug down into previous Mycenaean occupation levels, apparently without realization of their existence. To be sure, this sort of evidence for an arrival of Dorians in the Argolid does not prove that they arrived by sea. For this there is need of some kind of material evidence. This may be found, on the negative side, in the complete absence of any traces of Dorian occupation or passage along the overland corridor leading from southern Thessaly through Central Greece to the Peloponnese; and positively it may be forthcoming from a recent hypothesis on the origin of the pottery known to us as Protogeometric and universally regarded as the birthmark of the classic phase of Greek civilization.

In a previous study by Desborough, his well-known monograph on Protogeometric pottery, the position was taken that this originated in Attica, thereby leaving us with the unsolved problem how a long-established tradition such as that of Mycenaean vase decoration could have been transformed into a much more primitive, wholly unpictorial manner of ornament in a community that had never lost connexion with its Mycenaean past.

But now in his more recent work on *The Last Mycenaeans and their Successors*, from which I quoted liberally in my preceding lecture, Desborough is prepared to admit that recent investigation of Thessalian sites has lent colour to a rival thesis which derives the Protogeometric pottery style out of Thessaly, where (according to a Greek excavating archaeologist) it was developed without Mycenaean influence or contact. Consonant with this view, Protogeometric abstract linear ornamentation would have been imported from the north by the returning Heraklids with their Dorian contingents. From Argos it would have spread to Attica, there to undergo development and eventually become the accepted style for pottery through a great part of the Greek-speaking world. Argos would have remained influential in disseminating the style, perhaps most effectively so for Crete and Rhodes and the Dodecanese, inasmuch as these according to tradition were settled from Argos by a Heraklid leader named Althaimenes, who was of third-generation descent from Temenos, the Heraklid responsible for the reoccupation of Argos.

An interesting aspect of this novel theory on the Thessalian origin of the Protogeometric pottery style is its rehabilitation, after a couple of generations of complete rejection by modern thinking, of the old idea that Geometric vase design was a rude peasant style, a *Bauernstil,* brought by the Dorian invasion. To this doctrine there had been two capital objections: first, that the Geometric ceramic style had flourished most especially in Attica, a region never occupied by the Dorians; and secondly, that there were no discoverable traces of it along the route by which the Dorians traditionally entered the Peloponnese. Both of these observations are still sound; but they are irrelevant if we believe that Protogeometric reached Argos by sea and was disseminated thence by the Dorian newcomers, even as they themselves spread out through the nearby lands.

As they did so, they met with little opposition from the few inhabitants that had survived from Late Mycenaean days. The Heraklids had no need to conquer by force of arms a land so thinly populated that it had no power— and presumably no need or desire—to resist their arrival. So too in succeeding years, as the Doric folk increased and spread out over the nearby Aegean isles, there again it encountered no opposition because, like the Peloponnese, the south Aegean was well-nigh deserted. In a monograph on the island of Aegina Gabriel Welter held that it was uninhabited (*menschenleer*) after the

Mycenaean period; and Desborough asserts that the island of Melos had been abandoned by its Mycenaean inhabitants. Now at last, after having been shunned for centuries following its terrible disaster, Santorin was occupied once more and instead of its former name Kalliste was re-named Thera. The neighbouring islands, that had suffered only temporary damage from the great volcanic eruption and had recovered their prosperity during the Mycenaean age, had subsequently lost that prosperity and remained virtually empty until the Dorians came to re-settle them. Desborough, discussing the Dodecanesian island of Kos, was puzzled at finding 'no clue as to the cause of its final desertion' in Late Mycenaean times. 'There must have been some serious disaster', he decides; yet admits that 'no destruction is visible', adding that 'it can hardly be supposed that there was a complete depopulation, and yet there is no clear evidence of continuity into the Protogeometric period'. Quite the contrary! Since graves of late Protogeometric date have been found sunken into the site of a preceding Mycenaean settlement, there is—as Desborough freely admits—a definite instance of interruption of cultural continuity.

Despite the fact that there is no indication that the late Mycenaeans were driven out by any human intervention, they abandoned the south Aegean islands even as they deserted the central Peloponnese. For some reason and from some cause over which they had no control they found life in Greece and the southern Aegean so unendurable that they could not remain.

What forced them to evacuate their towns and villages?

The Key to the Riddle

In the seventh book of his *History* Herodotus recounts that Crete was so beset by famine and pestilence (λιμόν τε καὶ λοιμόν) after the Trojan War that it became virtually uninhabited (ἐρημωθεῖσα) until its resettlement by later inhabitants. Could Herodotus by any chance have had access to a true tradition? I remind you of the famine that overtook the Hittites around the year 1200 B.C. and of that other passage in Herodotus wherein he tells of a 'severe famine over all Lydia' that 'not relaxing but becoming an ever more powerful ill' for the space of eighteen years, forced half the population to emigrate to Italian Etruria.

Are such accounts to be trusted as actual history? And is it a credible supposition that it was famine that overwhelmed the Mycenaean civilization? Let us look at the matter dispassionately as a meteorological problem. For famine is caused by drought, and drought is a climatological condition.

I do not doubt that most of you have had experience of the hot Aegean summer with its cloudless skies from which oftentimes no drop of rain will fall between May and late September. Out on the Aegean in daytime during July and August the steady trade wind ploughs the bright blue sea into foam-topped waves. So strong is this wind that if one wishes to cross from one island to another— let us say, from Delos or Mykonos to nearby Tenos—the little Greek steamer can barely make headway against it. It is this wind that, solely and entirely, is responsible for the long rainless summers of the Aegean. As was explained in my introductory lecture, the trade wind is the southward returning draught of a great circulating air current that leaves the land rainless beneath it. Taking the eastern Mediterranean under its sway during the summer months, the trade wind blocks the passage for the Atlantic storms that bring wet summers to middle Europe but cannot penetrate the territory south of the Balkan mountain range.

Such is the present régime of the trade wind. But it would be an entirely legitimate question to ask whether this régime is fixed and permanent or has been subject to modification or even to outright change in the past. What, for example, would happen if there were a shift of latitude northward in the polar front against which the trade wind descends to begin its career? Of course, I cannot answer such a question with any confidence or show of conviction. In many respects meteorological speculation resembles the performances of the professional economists, who argue out an economic situation with admirable logic and intelligence, only to reach a conclusion diametrically opposite to the actual final outcome. So complex and so incalculable are the factors that determine climatic behaviour that, like the best-laid plans of mice and men, even the most authoritative meteorologists 'gang aft a-gley'.

At any rate it seems reasonably safe to say that any rise in planetary temperature, such as occurs at times (even though we have no satisfactory explanation of its cause), should produce a weakening of the high pressure polar front with a consequent further extension of the trade wind's operation northward into the temperate zone. Since the temperature gradient poleward from the equator would diminish, the trade wind's intensity might be lessened; but since the trade wind blows all the year round, it would still bring drought to the Aegean in summer, while in late spring and autumn it would, by virtue of its more northerly zone of passage, divert the cyclonic rain storms away from the Mediterranean track along which they now travel. There would result for southern Greece more nearly eight months of well-nigh continuous drought every year instead of the four or five that prevail at present. Such a climatic state would spell disaster to most living things in the course of only a few years, were it not for an ameliorating circumstance that would make existence possible in certain restricted regions, as I shall presently explain.

Lest in all this I seem to lean too heavily on my own meteorological incompetence, I turn for professional support to the proceedings of a conference of climatic experts held in 1952 and published under the general title of *Climatic Change*. In one of the communications to this symposium Dr H. W. Willett of the Massachusetts Institute of Technology read a paper on 'Atmospheric and Oceanic Circulation as Factors in Glacial–Interglacial Changes of Climate', in the course of which he discussed short-period climatic fluctuations since the last ice age with an average duration of about 1,850 years. He described these climatic phases as productive of 'a cycle of alternate expansion and contraction of the circumpolar vortex, with equatorward or poleward displacement of the prevailing storm tracks. Periods of contraction of the polar vortex [*sc.* during warm periods in the climatic cycle] are marked by warm characteristics, particularly in the higher latitudes, and by generally increased rainfall

poleward of latitude 50° N. and *decreased rainfall equatorward of this latitude*' (the italics are mine).

I take the foregoing quotation from Dr Willett to
signify that during a period of increased warmth such as
I assume to have prevailed during the thirteenth and
twelfth centuries B.C., the 'increased rainfall poleward of
latitude 50° North' would be due to a shift in the habitual
tracks of the cyclonic storms from the Mediterranean area
to northern Europe. Such a diversion would produce a
climatic deterioration in the Aegean zone by withdrawing
the present-day late autumn rains. In place of the cyclonic
storms that traverse the Mediterranean basin between the
months of November and March, the general eastward
drift of the earth's atmosphere would take over, bringing
for most of the year before and after the trade wind's
blowing only the steady westerly winds.

If you will grant me the supposition of such an atmospheric régime in the eastern Mediterranean, you will
have—I venture to assert—the key to the otherwise
puzzling phenomena of the Mycenaean migrations.

Whereas cyclonic storms with their veering vortices
overpass the mountain barriers in their path and are thus
able to penetrate the continental interior of Europe and
western Asia with their moisture-laden air, westerly winds
blowing over the Atlantic and entering the Mediterranean
through its western gap have a different action. After
picking up moisture from the sea, they tend to discharge
it again in the form of rain on striking any relatively high
transverse mountain barrier. Having shed part of their
moisture load on westward facing slopes, they pass without further discharge across the lower lying country

behind the mountain barrier. This is the well-known effect to which the term 'orographic rainfall' is applied. (*Orogenic* should be the proper word; but I cannot find it anywhere in use.) Presumably you have all encountered it in action somewhere on your travels.

It is well exemplified in my own country along the Pacific coast where rain falls on the western slopes of the Cascade mountains but leaves the interior land behind them dry and in many places outright desert. Farther north in the state of Washington the lofty Olympic range fronts the Pacific and so successfully drains the westerly sea-winds of their moisture that as much as 140 inches of rain may be deposited in the course of the year, while immediately behind this sky-flung obstacle there are strips of low-lying land that rank as the driest area on the whole west coast outside of southern California. Summer visitors to Scotland soon become painfully aware of the difference between westward and eastward exposure. In East Lothian the annual rainfall is recorded as averaging less than 30 inches; whereas farther west at picturesquely named Ballachulish there may be four times that amount, and on the crest of nearby Ben Nevis the annual precipitation may reach 150 inches—which makes $12\frac{1}{2}$ feet of solid water!

Let us apply these observations to Mediterranean conditions as we may imagine them in a climatic phase of dominant westerly winds. Consultation of a structural map of the Balkan peninsula will show that under a régime of orogenic rainfall the western shoreland of Greece from northern Messenia to Epirus should catch and condense the moisture-laden winds from the Ionian

Sea, even while southern Messenia, Laconia, and Argolis would be almost totally deprived of rain. (I remind you that the archaeological evidence indicates the abandonment of these interior and east-coast regions in Late Mycenaean times and at the same period an increased inhabitation of western Achaia.) The island of Kephallenia with its seaward exposure and its high central mountain would be a raincatch. (The ceramic evidence confirms this by attesting considerable migration thither.) Crete, however, would be in an unfortunate position. Had the long, fairly narrow, and very mountainous island been oriented north and south instead of west and east, it would have enjoyed abundant rainfall. As it lay, the westerly rain would have tended to pass it by, except on the high interior upland. (This may suggest why it was that—as Mr Hutchinson tells me—toward the close of Minoan times there was a general exodus from the coastal lowlands and a migration into the central heights.)

Beyond the Greek mainland the westerly winds, moving across the broad Aegean, would regain much of their moisture (though hardly in time to benefit the nearby Cyclades) bringing rain to the lofty islands of Chios, Ikaria, and Samos close to the Asia Minor coast and watering the less elevated continental shore by condensing moisture on the interior upland girdle of heights and ridges to feed the uniformly westward running rivers. On this view the Ionian migration from the Greek to the Asiatic mainland may be understood as nothing more mysterious than a flight from a drought-ridden to a better-watered land.

But the interior plateau of Asia Minor beyond the

rainshed of the broken Phrygian upland would have fared no better than the Peloponnese for rain—or perhaps even more poorly, because the high mountain walls shutting it off on either hand, north and south, would have contributed to turning the heart of Asia Minor into desert wasteland. So it was that the Hittites were forced to move out.

The preceding sketch of climatic conditions in Late Mycenaean and immediately subsequent time is in exact agreement with the archaeological evidence for the movements and density distribution of the human population in Greece and the Aegean, except for one seemingly serious flaw in the picture. That flaw is Attica. Being the easternmost canton of mainland Greece, it should have been (one might object) most of all subjected to the effects of drought. Yet tradition maintains that it was continuously inhabited from Mycenaean into classic times; and we have no reason for challenging the tradition.

On closer inspection this apparently fatal objection to my thesis of climatic calamity at the end of the Mycenaean age turns out to be its most striking confirmation. For the hundred-mile Gulf of Corinth, extending east from its gaping mouth in Patras Bay, is so shut in on either flank by high mountains that it acts as a gigantic funnel for westerly winds. These pick up moisture from the sea's surface as they pass over it, and this warm wet air is then channelled through the Aigosthena gap beneath Mount Cithaeron, to be condensed into rain as it is forced up the cooling heights of Parnes, Pentelikon, and Hymettos. Thus, granted a régime of prevailing westerlies, while the rest of eastern Greece was dry, the interior of Attica, the *mesogaia*, would be blest with rain.

Thucydides' claim that Attica escaped conquest by the Dorians because the land was not worth taking, so thin and unfertile was its soil, rings singularly false. It not only disagrees with present-day conditions, but it runs expressly counter to Plato's assertion in the *Critias* that the country bordered on the north by Cithaeron and Parnes and the district around Oropos 'is superior to all other land in fertility . . . in proof of which, this region is a match for any other soil in its range of fine harvests and its pasturage for all sorts of animals'. And no reader of Aristophanes can have missed his praise of the ease of Attic country life with its rich farms and orchards and vineyards. The simple truth is this: the Attic land was never occupied by the Dorians because it was never abandoned by its proper inhabitants, who had abundant reason for continuing to dwell in it.

This singularly fortunate land became a place of refuge for others driven out of their desiccating fields and pastures. The Heraklids abode there for a while before moving north through Thessaly. Migrants from Nestor's Pylos settled there, where some of them remained to become kings of Athens (according to legend), while others helped to lead the Ionian migration oversea. To judge by the motley composition of this emigrant throng which, if we may trust Herodotus, included Abantes from Euboea, Minyans from Orchomenos, Cadmeans from Thebes, Phocians, Arcadians, and Epidaurians— Attica had become a gathering place for the climatically dispossessed from most of eastern and central Greece.

The Key to the Riddle

This, then, is my interpretation of the archaeological evidence coupled with ancient oral tradition: a 'time of trouble' was occasioned by climatic causes that brought persistent drought with its attendant famine to most of mainland Greece; and it was this unlivable condition of their native abode that forced the Mycenaeans to emigrate, ending their century-long prosperity.

Although I have advanced this hypothesis for more than a decade, I could not conceal from myself that it was unsupported by any pertinent parallel from present-day meteorological records of drought induced by a similar climatic condition. Consequently, while not given to rejoicing in my fellow-man's misfortunes, I could not help feeling gratified at the severe drought that beset a large sector of my own country during the summer of 1964, since it offered indisputable evidence of calamity resulting from the substitution of persistent westerlies for the normal routine sequence of cyclonic low and anti-cyclonic high pressure areas. In agreement with typical orographic behaviour, the region west of the Pacific coastal range experienced unusually heavy rainfall at the very time that the interior country east of the Rocky Mountains suffered from the worst drought in thirty-five years. Our Weather Bureau's climatological laboratory announced that the persistence of westerly winds was uniquely responsible for this condition, even though it would not commit itself to any sure explanation of the cause of this departure from the normal weather pattern.

Again, during the following summer, after these lectures were delivered, the spectre of oncoming drought stalked our eastern seaboard as the great cities watched their reservoirs shrink to ever lower water levels. Although there is little likelihood that New York will ever become unlivable for lack of water, the prospect of the possibility of such a calamity brought shudders to millions of its citizens and sent its local authorities into alarmed consultation.

I very much doubt whether anyone who has always lived in this well-watered isle of Britain can have any conception of the horrors of enduring total drought, with its pitiless lingering torture in which all men and animals and growing plants and trees alike must wane and wither and die. I owe to one of my Cambridge audience the following, perhaps somewhat over-dramatically written, yet essentially quite accurate, account of drought in an unhappy province of north-east Brazil:

In the dry season the *sertão* looks like the burnt land of the prophets. You would have thought that fire had passed over it and burnt up all its greenery. Throughout the vast plain, which extends farther than the eye can see, solitary and naked trees raise their stiff and twisted branches, looking like the fleshless bones of the old forest. The grass that once covered the earth with a green carpet has been gnawed down to the roots by the famished animals and reduced to a thick ashen layer, which the slightest gust of wind whirls into a grey cloud.

The blazing sun filters a few dull rays down to the scorched earth and clothes with a dusty and leaden shroud the skeletons of the trees lined one behind another in mournful file.

The air, formerly full of noisy birds with their brilliant plumage shining in the light, is now as empty and silent as the earth, cleft only by the heavy flight of the vultures scenting carrion.

The Key to the Riddle

From time to time a crackling of twigs may be heard. It is the cattle wandering through this ghost of a forest. A little farther on, they will fall and die, desiccated by thirst rather than weakened by hunger.[1]

From a different writer, but referring to the same dreadful Brazilian drought, I excerpt the following, thinking it still more significant for our problem of depopulation and destruction in Late Mycenaean times:

During the great famine of 1877 epidemic disease killed 50% of the population, a matter of half a million persons. Even in fairly normal periods the effects of drought in one way or another will eliminate half of the newborn children within their first—and only—year of life. When the drought persists in strength through three consecutive years, the inhabitants have so little prospect of survival that they emigrate in great numbers to climatically more fortunate regions. As recently as 1953, according to official statistics, 286 000 left the drought-stricken area. But even this draining off of hungry mouths is not enough to alleviate existence for those who remain behind. In this same year of 1953, following three preceding years of unremitting drought, the people of the burnt-out countryside descended *en masse*, armed with every available weapon, to sack and pillage the settlements where any food had been stored. Always [says this writer] there comes a time, a homicidal moment, when the famished cannot longer endure the sight of the well-nourished. Kinsman and friend alike must succumb to their desperation.[2]

In view of this final resort to violence by a drought-stricken people, it should be pertinent to point out that under the Mycenaean system of economy the palaces of

1 Translated from José de Alencar, *O Sertanejo*.
2 Translated from Pierre Joffroy, *Brésil* (in *Collection Petite Planète*) (Éditions du Seuil, Paris, 1958).

the regional kings were not only their dwelling places, but served also as storerooms for the edible provender that they collected from their dependants. Perhaps we need not look further for the incendiary fate that overtook the centres of Mycenaean civilization.

It frequently occurs that when a period of drought finally breaks, it is succeeded by a compensatory onset of unusually heavy rains. I quote a vivid description of such a sequence of abnormal dry and wet that took place only four years ago in equatorial Africa:

In Kenya in 1961 the 'long rains' of March to June failed to arrive, with disastrous results for the wild animals; grazing areas and water holes dried up and thousands of them died. The 'short rains' of October to December thereupon arrived in such insane force and abundance that many animals that had not died of thirst died of drowning. Bridges and roads were washed away, dams burst and power stations were wrecked. The disaster spread through much of East Africa, until an estimated million people were in danger of starvation. They had to be saved by air-drops of food and an international relief programme . . . Obviously, if there were many such drought–flood cycles as that of 1961, there would be nobody left to enjoy Kenya's generally attractive climate.

A similar picture, though on much minuter scale, is drawn in the eighteenth chapter of the First Book of Kings, wherein a three-year drought brought 'sore famine in Samaria', so that it became hard to 'find grass to save the horses and mules alive', until at last Elijah went to the top of Mount Carmel, having gathered Israel together to look for rain.

And he [Elijah] said to his servant, Go up now, look toward the sea. And he went up, and looked, and said, There is nothing. And he said, Go again seven times. And it came to pass at the seventh time that he said, Behold, there ariseth a little cloud out of the sea, as small as a man's hand . . . And it came to pass in a little while, that the heaven grew black with clouds and wind, and there was a great rain.

Perhaps it is mere coincidence that the breaking of the three-year drought at the prophet's praying is to be dated to the second quarter of the ninth century before Christ. Yet this is precisely the time when the protracted phase of drought in the eastern Mediterranean seems to have been succeeded by a colder and much wetter climate. Yet the onset could not have been entirely abrupt, even though the archaeological evidence yields no indication of a resumption of a more livable climatic régime earlier than the ninth century. Still, the return of the Heraklids to their ancestral realm argues an amelioration of the drought to make possible their return. Unfortunately we do not know when this event took place, unless we may argue from the incidence of Protogeometric vases that it should be dated somewhat later than the year 1000 B.C.

Some sort of widespread and very marked climatic change accompanying the onset of classical Greek culture might have been deduced from various more general considerations such as the shift in costume from the semi-nude Minoan and Mycenaean attire to the heavier classical raiment or, in architecture, the change from flat to pitched gable roofs, indicative of heavy rainfall. But as far as I can discover—if we disregard Elijah's exploit as fortuitous—the only written record of the reversal from drought to rain concerns the Nile valley, where great floods occurred in the eighth and early seventh centuries B.C. For the third year of the reign of Osorkon III (which is to say 776 B.C., the very year assigned to the first Olympiad in Greece) it is recorded in Egyptian historical records that the Nile lapped the desert cliffs 'like the beginning of the world', breaking all the dykes, engulfing men in their towns 'like sandflies', and converting to marshland the precincts of the Theban temples, so that when the statue of the god was carried in procession at the festival of Amon 'the people were like swimmers'. During the reign of Ethiopian Shabaka at the close of the eighth century the Delta was repeatedly flooded, if we may make this inference from the statement in Herodotus (II. 137) that instead of putting to death offenders against the law, 'Sabakōs ordered them to heap earth against their towns. In this way the towns were made higher.' Again in 683 B.C., in the sixth year of the reign of Taharka 'the land was like the sea, the sands disappeared, and water inundated the city of Thebes. There is nothing comparable in our ancestral annals: it was a great rain in Nubia that caused it.' So runs the hieroglyphic inscription, and there is no reason for doubting its veracity.

It may seem peculiar that an onset of abnormally wet weather over central and southern Europe, such as the meteorologists ascribe to the ninth and eighth centuries B.C., should have synchronized with abnormal floods in Egypt. The annual rising of the Nile is in no way dependent on the trade wind's passage down the Red Sea nor yet on cyclonic activity over the Mediterranean. The explanation must be found in the heightening of the general atmospheric circulation during a planetary cold phase, by virtue of which there would have been increased transportation of evaporated equatorial Atlantic water across Central Africa, to be precipitated as rain on the lofty Ethiopian mountain barrier. If this assumption is correct, it would follow conversely that during the preceding warm planetary phase that brought drought to the Aegean, the annual supply of silt-bearing water for the Egyptian fields would have been curtailed; so that the cultural disintegration in the late Ramessid and Tanite period may have had an economic rather than a political or social cause. With the resumption of high Nile floods fertility was restored to Egypt and the kingdom regained its prosperity.

In Europe a spectacular proof of the onset of abnormally heavy rains at about the same period as the great Nile floods might be deduced from the Swiss lakedwellings and the north-Italian *terremare,* if only we could be certain that (as has been persuasively argued by the Swedish scholar, Säflund) the inhabitants of these strange settlements were seeking to escape the effects of too much water rather than perversely exploiting an aqueous mode of existence. In any case, an aggravated pluvial phase about the mid-millennium is proven by the destruction through inundation and the consequent abandonment of many of the Swiss lake villages. A comparable index of changing climatic conditions has been derived from the state of cultural intercourse and commercial exchange over the alpine passes. Your distinguished climatologist, the late C. E. P. Brooks, concluded from the archaeological evidence that open communication in the Alps reached a maximum between 1200 and 900 B.C. (which, I may remind you, was the drought phase that I have tried to establish for the eastern

Mediterranean), whereas he deduced a climatic reversal to a much colder and wetter phase after 900, arguing that the demonstrable fact that the alpine valley settlements of the Late Hallstatt period developed in complete isolation indicated an onset of heavy snowfall accompanied by glacial expansion. In this connexion notice should be taken of the surprising observation that near the end of the Hallstatt period the level of the Lake of Constance rose some thirty feet.

Even more spectacular, but somewhat insecure chronologically, is the inference from circumstantial evidence that the Hungarian plain, an immense tract of comparatively low-lying land in which a number of large rivers converge, must have become almost totally submerged early in the first millennium B.C. How else shall we explain the fact that the rich and active phase of the Hungarian Bronze Age known to archaeologists as Bronze IV and dated by Åberg as lasting from about 1000 to about 850 B.C. (the drought period in Greece!) met, in Åberg's words, 'an unexpected and sudden end ... after which the country is without any discoverable sign of occupation and seems deserted'? This is the exact antithesis of what I have been claiming happened in Mycenaean Greece—there, flight from a waterless land; here, flight from overwhelming flood.

There is thus pretty sound circumstantial evidence that throughout southern Europe and the Mediterranean there had been a shift to a colder and wetter climate during the ninth century B.C., culminating at about the middle of the first millennium B.C. We cannot hope to plot its incidence or trace its career very precisely. Perhaps all that we can safely say is, if the Heraklids found southern Greece climatically liveable when they returned with their Dorian following, around the year 1000 B.C., the drought must have already begun to relent at that time; but the real onset of colder climate with abundant autumn and spring rain did not eventuate until a century later. By the time of the first Olympiad, in 776 B.C., from which the classical world dated its historical career, a climatic change had restored fertility to continental Greece.

Now, there is a certain amount of statistical evidence to encourage the belief that a sudden increase in a community's food supply will occasion a corresponding increase in reproduction of the population. This increased rate will persist for a time, then fall off to a somewhat lower but constant level. Judging from the sudden remarkable outburst of emigration from the Aegean basin to southern Italy, Sicily, and the Black Sea shoreland, such a condition, amounting virtually to a 'population explosion', developed in Greece. Based on the recorded foundation dates for the various colonies, emigration began shortly after the middle of the eighth century, gained momentum throughout the seventh, tapered off in the sixth, and ceased thereafter to be an important element in the Greek ecology. The brusque climatic reversal that I have been postulating for the mid-ninth century may be in direct causal relation to this phenomenon.

If we may place any reliance on the suggestion made by several of our climatologists that there is a recurrent climatic swing conforming to a period of about 1,850 years, then, by calculating forward and backward from the ninth century B.C., we should encounter a cold and stormy phase at about the year A.D. 1000 and an earlier one at about 2700 B.C. Perhaps it is a mere coincidence—but if so, it is a very striking one—that the later of the two dates, the opening of the eleventh Christian century, coincides quite closely with the ending of the Dark Ages in Europe as well as with the resurgence of Byzantine power in the Near East; while the earlier date, 2700 B.C., is that now pretty confidently upheld for the emergence of enlightened civilization in Egypt under Zoser, the first of the great pyramid builders, and synchronously in Sumer under the First Dynasty of Ur.

If, for the contrary swing of the climatic pendulum toward drought, we take the year 1200 B.C. as our point of departure and count 1,850 years forward and back therefrom, we should encounter a disastrous drought phase in the eastern Mediterranean around 3000 B.C. (as to which we are at present ill-informed, but in which there is some slight reason to believe), and again another in the seventh century of our era (about which it is possible to speculate with much greater assurance). I am only too well aware that the disintegration of the classical Greco-Roman civilization in and after the fourth century of our era is a problem of great complexity, far beyond my limited competence, and involving so many considerations that the climatological factor can at most be only a contributory cause. I shall therefore limit myself, in closing these lectures, to drawing attention to the most significant parallel between the breakdown of Greek civilization in the Mycenaean age and that in Byzantine times after an intervening phase of cultural prosperity that had persisted for more than a thousand years.

The Key to the Riddle

The invasion of Greece by Slavic people during the seventh and eighth centuries of our era is an historic event as heavily cloaked in mystery as the incursion of the Dorians some seventeen or eighteen hundred years earlier, and constitutes a theme for debate every whit as varyingly interpreted by modern historians, who have tended to be vehement partisans of totally opposing views. For some —among whom I may cite the notorious Fallmerayer of the 1830s and for more recent times A. Philippson and M. Vasmer—Greece was so strongly overrun by the Slavic invaders as to alter profoundly its ethnic and social composition; whereas for others—most notably those of Hellenic speech moved by patriotic indignation—this incursion of the Slavs was a negligible incident that occasioned no vital or distinguishable change in the population, biologically or otherwise. Such completely contradictory opinions could be maintained because the Byzantine chronicles are indecisive, the linguistic evidence is ambiguous, and there did not seem to be any other source of information. But more recently—as in the case of the Mycenaean debacle—archaeology has stepped in and supplied new data on which to base more confident conclusions. You will recall that the archaeological evidence for the end of the Mycenaean period was almost entirely ceramic. Now, for the Greek Middle Ages, it is equally restrictedly numismatic and architectural. To be sure, it must be granted that both these latter sources are largely of a negative sort; but archaeologists have learned to treat negative evidence as positive information, if handled critically and discreetly.

As an example of this sort of conclusion *e nihilo* it is

argued that many Greek sites in the Peloponnese were vacated by their inhabitants at a date earlier than any Slavic incursion into southern Greece because (to cite some typical instances) Gortys in Arcadia, known to have been unoccupied in later medieval times, has yielded no coins later than the mid-fifth century of our era; again, Arcadian Orchomenos has produced coins of Justinian and Justin II and, of much later date, coins of Constantine Porphyrogennetos, but none from the intervening period between the sixth and the tenth century. Again, at Olympia on the ruins of the sacred Altis, ravaged by the Goths and destroyed by earthquake, there arose an unpretentious village in the sixth century. In this there have been found Byzantine coins of various emperors from Constantine to the close of the sixth century; but shortly after the year 600 they cease abruptly, the latest being from the reign of Phokas, 602–10. At this date the village seems to have disappeared totally, the site remaining unoccupied thereafter until modern times. Just as in the Late Mycenaean era Peloponnesian settlements were abandoned long before the Dorians set foot on their soil, so here in the Middle Ages the population was moving out from localities that the Slavs did not reach until two or three centuries later. The exodus is clearly substantiated by casual mention by the Byzantine chroniclers, notably in the Monemvasía Chronicle, of Greek shifts of population from Corinth to the island of Aegina, from Argos to the Cyclades, on the west coast from Patras to Calabria in southern Italy, and in the interior of the Peloponnese from Laconia to Demena in Sicily. If the Mycenaean *diaspora* is thus repeated in the early Middle

Ages, the return of the Heraklids to their native land is paralleled by the Monemvasia Chronicle's reference to a return to Patras by the descendants of those who had migrated to Italy some 200 years earlier and the further notation of a recolonization of Lacedaemon. I venture to suggest that this is an indication that by the ninth century a period of destructive drought had come to an end and southern Greece was once more fit to support an increasing population.

I have time only for casual citation of the architectural evidence as M. Antoine Bon presents it in his illuminating monograph.[1] 'As far as I know,' he writes, 'not a single monument appears to have been built in the Peloponnese between the seventh and the ninth century. At least, I myself have never come across or seen mentioned any structure that can certainly be assigned to this intervening period.' Yet this cannot be due to the arrival of the Slavs on the scene, about whose coming M. Bon ventures to assert that it 'did not have the character of a military conquest', but of an infiltration, without combat, of disconnected groups of nomadic shepherd folk, moving in with their wives, children, and household possessions to occupy a half-empty countryside. This is precisely the picture that I entertain for the coming of the Dorians after the Mycenaean dispersal. Since history repeats itself only when identical conditions prevail, the Slavic invasion of the eighth century after Christ repeats the Dorian invasion, eighteen centuries earlier, because in both events a depopulating drought was succeeded by

[1] *Le Péloponnèse Byzantin jusqu'en 1204* (Presses Universitaires de France, Paris, 1951).

climatic amelioration permitting resettlement of the deserted area. A similar parallel may be drawn to the abandonment of the central Anatolian plateau by the Hittites and, after two or three hundred years, the re-occupation of the interior of Asia Minor by Phrygians moving in from more northerly Balkan territory. The Phrygians did not destroy the Hittites any more than the Dorians destroyed the Mycenaean Greeks.

In thus interpreting the phenomena of cultural discontinuity in the nearer East I am reminded of Shelley's marvellous lines in which

> Life like a dome of many-coloured glass
> Stains the white radiance of eternity.

Historians, too, when they view the long past, dissolve its white light into a set of rainbow colours according as they peer through their glasses of political, economic, geographic and geophysical, or anthropological interpretation. Only when the broken colours are reblended will the white light of historic actuality shine out. For these lectures I have been looking through some very restrictive lenses; but I submit, in closing, that the perhaps unfamiliar hue that they have cast over Mycenaean and medieval Greece is no merely random colouring, but a physically actual component of the clear light of truth.